The Tyndale Old Testament Commentaries

General Editor: Professor D. J. Wiseman, O.B.E., M.A., D.Lit., F.B.A., F.S.A

THE PROVERBS

THE PROVERBS

AN INTRODUCTION AND COMMENTARY

by

THE REV. DEREK KIDNER, M.A.
Warden, Tyndale House, Cambridge

INTER-VARSITY PRESS

© 1964 by The Tyndale Press, Leicester, England. Published in America by
InterVarsity Press, Downers Grove, Illinois, with permission from Inter-Varsity
Fellowship, England.

InterVarsity Press is the book-publishing division of Inter-Varsity Christian Fellowship,
a student movement active on campus at hundreds of universities, colleges
and schools of nursing. For information about local and regional activities, write
IVCF, 233 Langdon St., Madison, WI 53703.

Distributed in Canada through InterVarsity Press, 1875 Leslie St., Unit 10,
Don Mills, Ontario M3B 2M5, Canada.

ISBN paper 0-87784-266-3
ISBN cloth 0-87784-861-0
Library of Congress Catalog Card Number: 75-23850

Printed in the United States of America

21	20	19	18	17	16	15	14	13	12	11	10	9	8
93	92	91	90	89	88	87	86	85	84	83	82	81	

GENERAL PREFACE

THE welcome accorded to the series of *Tyndale New Testament Commentaries*, and many requests, encourage us to present further volumes intended to cover all the books of the Old Testament.

The aim of this series is to provide the student of the Bible with a handy, up-to-date commentary on each book, with the primary emphasis on exegesis. Major critical questions are discussed in the introductions and additional notes, while undue technicalities have been avoided. The length of some Old Testament books precludes detailed treatment if these volumes are to be kept to a moderate length and price, yet comment intended to stimulate devotional thought is not entirely excluded, for the sake of both student and preacher.

While all are united in their belief in the divine inspiration, essential trustworthiness and practical relevance of the sacred writings, individual authors have freely made their own contributions. No detailed uniformity of method has been imposed in the handling of books of such varied subject matter, form and style as the Old Testament.

In the Old Testament in particular no single English translation is adequate to reflect the original text. The authors of these commentaries therefore freely quote various versions, or give their own translation, in the endeavour to make the more difficult passages or words meaningful today. Where necessary, words from the Hebrew (and Aramaic) Massoretic Text underlying their studies are transliterated. This will help the reader who may be unfamiliar with the Semitic languages to identify the word under discussion and thus to follow the argument. Others will observe that these transliterations follow a well-recognized pattern (as used, for example, in *The New Bible Dictionary*, 1962). It is assumed throughout that the reader will have ready access to one, or more, reliable rendering of the Bible in English.

GENERAL PREFACE

There are signs of a renewed interest in the meaning and message of the Old Testament and it is hoped that this series will thus further the systematic study of the revelation of God and His will and ways as seen in these records. It is the prayer of the editor and publisher, as of the authors, that these books will help many to understand, and to respond to, the Word of God today.

D. J. WISEMAN.

CONTENTS

AUTHOR'S PREFACE

'WHEN words are many, transgression is not lacking'; when they are sixty thousand, a preface will do nothing to mend matters. But I wish to thank those who have drawn my attention to various notes and studies of matters in Proverbs which I would otherwise have overlooked. In student days my feet were first set on this path by Professor D. W. Thomas, to my great benefit; but he must not be thought responsible for their erratic progress. In more recent times I have also enjoyed the stimulus and advice of members of the Old Testament Group of the Tyndale Fellowship, especially Professor D. J. Wiseman and Mr. K. A. Kitchen – but they too must be cleared of complicity in my conclusions, which are my own.

The reader is asked to bear with discussions which sometimes become a little technical, since the meaning of the text must be even a short commentary's first concern. But to balance this attention to detail I have included two aids to navigation, by which the length and breadth of Proverbs may be more easily explored. The first is a set of subject-studies in which the teaching scattered throughout the book, on eight leading topics, is brought together; the second is a short concordance, which may perhaps serve the double purpose of locating lost sayings (in territory notoriously hard to search) and providing the beginnings of further subject-studies. By such means, may the neglected wealth of the Proverbs find its way into many new hands.

DEREK KIDNER.

CHIEF ABBREVIATIONS

AASOR	*Annual of the American Schools of Oriental Research.*
ANET	*Ancient Near Eastern Texts*[2] by J. B. Pritchard, 1955.
AV	English Authorized Version (King James).
BDB	*Hebrew-English Lexicon of the Old Testament* by Brown, Driver and Briggs, 1907.
BWL	*Babylonian Wisdom Literature* by W. G. Lambert, 1960.
DOTT	*Documents from Old Testament Times* edited by D. W. Thomas, 1958.
E.T.	English Translation.
Fritsch	See *IB*, below.
Heb.	Hebrew.
IB	*Interpreter's Bible*, Vol. 4 (Psalms, Proverbs), 1955: Exegesis by C. T. Fritsch.
ICC	*International Critical Commentary: Proverbs* by C. H. Toy, 1899.
JBL	*Journal of Biblical Literature.*
JEA	*Journal of Egyptian Archaeology.*
JTS	*Journal of Theological Studies.*
KB	*Lexicon in Veteris Testamenti Libros* by Köhler-Baumgartner, 1953.
Knox	The Old Testament Newly Translated from the Latin Vulgate by Ronald A. Knox, 1949.
LXX	The Septuagint (pre-Christian Greek version of the Old Testament).
Martin	*Proverbs (etc.) (Century Bible)*, 1908: Commentary by G. C. Martin.
mg	Margin.
Moffatt	A New Translation of the Bible by James Moffatt, 1935.
MT	Massoretic Text.
NBC	*The New Bible Commentary* edited by F. Davidson, A. Stibbs, E. Kevan, 1953.

CHIEF ABBREVIATIONS

Oesterley	See *WC*, below.
OTMS	*The Old Testament and Modern Study* edited by H. H. Rowley, 1951.
OTS	*Oudtestamentische Studiën.*
RV	English Revised Version, 1885.
RSV	American Revised Standard Version, 1952.
SP	*Sumerian Proverbs* by E. I. Gordon, 1959.
Syr.	*The Peshitta* (Translation of the Old Testament into Syriac).
Targ.	*The Targums* (Translation of the Old Testament into Aramaic).
Toy	See *ICC*, above.
Vulg.	The Vulgate (Translation of the Bible into Latin, by Jerome).
VT	*Vetus Testamentum.*
WC	*Westminster Commentaries: Proverbs* by W.O.E. Oesterley, 1929.
WIANE	*Wisdom in Israel and in the Ancient Near East* edited by M. Noth and D. W. Thomas, 1955.
ZAW	*Zeitschrift für die alttestamentliche Wissenschaft.*

INTRODUCTION

'MAKE the bad people good, and the good people nice', is supposed to have been a child's prayer: it makes the point, with proverbic brevity, that there are details of character small enough to escape the mesh of the law and the broadsides of the prophets, and yet decisive in personal dealings. Proverbs moves in this realm, asking what a person is like to live with, or to employ; how he manages his affairs, his time and himself. This good lady, for instance – does she talk too much? That cheerful soul – is he bearable in the early morning? And this friend who is always dropping in – here is some advice for him . . . and for that rather aimless lad . . .

But it is not a portrait-album or a book of manners: it offers a key to life. The samples of behaviour which it holds up to view are all assessed by one criterion, which could be summed up in the question, 'Is this wisdom or folly?' This is a unifying approach to life, because it suits the most commonplace realms as fully as the most exalted. Wisdom leaves its signature on anything well made or well judged, from an apt remark to the universe itself, from a shrewd policy (which springs from practical insight) to a noble action (which presupposes moral and spiritual discernment). In other words, it is equally at home in the realms of nature and art, of ethics and politics, to mention no others, and forms a single basis of judgment for them all.

Such an approach could have the effect of lowering everything to a common level, if wisdom were equated with selfish calculation. There *is* calculation in Proverbs, for there is every encouragement to count the cost or reward of one's actions, and to study the ways of getting things done; but wisdom as taught here is God-centred, and even when it is most down-to-earth it consists in the shrewd and sound handling of one's affairs in *God's* world, in submission to His will.[1]

Proverbs does not stand alone. A particular group in Israel studied life from this angle, and was recognizable as one of the three main channels of revelation. There was a saying, quoted in Jeremiah 18:18, that 'The law shall not perish from the priest, nor counsel from the wise, nor the word from the prophet'; and the tone of voice of this second group can be heard in some of the Psalms, but especially in the three 'Wisdom Books' of the Old Testament: Job, Proverbs and Ecclesiastes. In these two companion-volumes to Proverbs the emphasis moves away from statements to questions – or, to put it another way, from asking the questions that begin with 'What?' ('What are the qualities of a fine wife?', 'What are the dangers of loose living?', and so on) to asking those that begin with 'How?' and 'Why?' – questions about the ways of God and the purpose of life.

The wisdom tradition lived on in Judaism, leaving its most notable deposits in two books to be found in the Apocrypha: Ecclesiasticus (more conveniently known by its author's name, Ben-Sira) and The Wisdom of Solomon. Ben-Sira (*c.* 180 BC) stands in the tradition of Proverbs, but is more discursive and more distinctly Jewish. The Wisdom of Solomon (first century BC) is further-ranging than Ben-Sira, particularly in developing the theme of the personified wisdom of Proverbs 8, for which it uses language that is partly an anticipation of the New Testament's Christological terms, and partly what might be called a platonic flirtation with Greek thought. It was soon to be outdone, in the latter respect, by the Alexandrian Jew, Philo.

But we can also trace the wisdom element in Israel back to early times. Before Solomon gave it the immense stimulus of his own genius and of the inflow of foreign talent, there were permanent counsellors at his father's court (1 Ch. 27:32, 33), and unofficial reputations which spread far. We meet the wise

[1] This point is discussed further in the subject-study: God and Man, pp. 31ff.

14

woman of Tekoa in 2 Samuel 14, and another one from Abel in 20:16ff. who claimed that the town itself was famous for its counsel. And there is better evidence than reputations, for there are sayings that have survived from those times in the characteristic styles of wisdom. David quoted a 'proverb (*māšāl*) of the ancients' (1 Sa. 24:13), Samson propounded his riddle (*ḥiḍâ*; Jdg. 14:14; *cf.* Pr. 1:6), Jotham his fable (Jdg. 9:8ff.) – a favourite form in the ancient world – and Nathan his parable (2 Sa. 12:1ff.). Most of these examples are beautifully formed: the craftsmanship is eloquent proof of the vigour of a living tradition.

We can also ask how wide a movement this was. Some rivalry has been suspected between the prophets and this school, and certainly there are some prophetic blasts against the wise (*e.g.* Is. 29:14; Je. 8:8). But there was no real clash of interests; the men who were denounced were misusing their powers, as the false prophets and priests misused theirs. True wisdom and true prophecy both started from the fear of the Lord, and both worked hard to make Israel *think*. It was a prophet who said 'My people are destroyed for lack of knowledge'; and he was echoed by his fellows (Ho. 4:6; *cf.* Is. 1:3; 5:13; Je. 4:22; *etc.*). It was, fittingly, a sage – Solomon himself – who said about prophecy, 'Where there is no vision, the people run wild' (Pr. 29:18). Even the techniques of the wise were used in prophecy: *cf.* the striking sequence beginning with 'Shall two walk together. . . ?', in Amos 3:3–8, and several terms and passages in Jeremiah (*e.g.* 17:5ff.).[1]

To go further still, we may see wisdom as a thread running through the whole fabric of the Old Testament. Because God is self-consistent, what He wills can always be expressed as what wisdom dictates, and the themes of history, law, prophecy and apocalyptic can all be transposed into this key. The fall of man was a choosing of what bid fair 'to make one wise' (Gn. 3:6) but flouted the first principle of wisdom, the fear of the Lord. By contrast, the last portrait in Genesis is the living image of

[1] See further J. Lindblom, 'Wisdom in the Old Testament Prophets', in *WIANE*, pp. 192ff.

the wise man of Proverbs, in the person of Joseph, who (to quote G. von Rad[1]) 'through discipline, modesty, knowledge, self-mastery and the fear of God (Gn. 42:18) had given a noble form to his whole being. . . . Before Pharaoh he proves himself a shrewd counsellor, and before his brothers the man who can be silent, . . . and finally the one who "covered up all sins with love" (Pr. 10:12)'. Again, Deuteronomy presents the law as 'your wisdom and your understanding in the sight of the peoples' (Dt. 4:6), and sets before Israel the same two ways, of life and death, which are a favourite theme of Proverbs. Apocalypse is no exception, displaying human destiny mapped out by divine wisdom, and the map read by the wise (Dn. 2:20, 21; 12:10). In the age to come it is again the wise who will 'shine as the brightness of the firmament'; and this is but another term for those 'that turn many to righteousness' (Dn. 12:3).

Nor, finally, should we stop with the old covenant. A greater than Solomon was to come, choosing to teach in the forms and rhythms of the wise, and carrying their *māšāl*[2] to its ultimate perfection in His parables. As for His Person, while the New Testament took up the language of the Law and the Prophets to describe His office among His people, as Prophet, Priest and King, it turned to Proverbs (see 8:22ff.) and to the thought-forms of the wise for terms to express His relation to the universe and His one-ness with the Father, as the One in whom all things were created and consist, in whom lie hidden all the treasures of wisdom and knowledge; Christ, in fact, as the Wisdom of God.

II. WISDOM IN THE ANCIENT WORLD

The Bible often alludes to the wisdom and wise men of Israel's neighbours, particularly those of Egypt (Acts 7:22; 1 Ki. 4:30 (MT, 5:10); Is. 19:11,12), of Edom and Arabia (Je. 49:7;

---

[1] *Old Testament Theology* (E.T. 1962), I, p. 432.
[2] For this term, see commentary on 1:1; for the application of it to our Lord's parables, *cf.* Mt. 13:35 with Ps. 78:2.

Ob. 8; Jb. 1:3; 1 Ki. 4:30), of Babylon (Is. 47:10; Dn. 1:4, 20, *etc.*) and of Phoenicia (Ezk. 28:3ff.; Zc. 9:2). While the Old Testament scorns the magic and superstition which debased much of this thought (Is. 47:12,13), and the pride which inflated it (Jb. 5:13), it can speak of the gentile sages with a respect it never shows towards their priests and prophets. Solomon outstripped them, but we are expected to be impressed by the fact; and Daniel excelled the wise men of Babylon as one who stood at the head of their own profession (Dn. 5:11, 12). Admittedly it was God who gave supernatural insight to these Israelites; but the Old Testament clearly implies that a man can still think validly and talk wisely, within a limited field, without special revelation. This is put beyond doubt by the story of Ahithophel, whose advice continued to be 'as if a man inquired at the oracle of God', even after he had turned traitor (2 Sa. 16:23; 17:14).

The rapid spread of Solomon's reputation, and the flocking of foreign visitors to hear him (1 Ki. 4:34; 10:1–13,24), illustrate the intellectual climate of the time both outside and within Israel. It was a common thing for sages to visit foreign courts and test each other's wit and wisdom. If Solomon paid no visits in return, at least there was an interest aroused at his court in comparing his sayings with the words of his visitors (1 Ki. 4:30,31), and Proverbs shows by its contents that Israel's wise men were ready to sift and assimilate some of this imported wealth (see below, Structure and Authorship, pp. 22ff.).

Enough of this ancient wisdom has survived to give us an idea of its main interests and its quality, and it is clear at once that it was seeking (among other things) answers to the very questions that occupy the biblical wisdom books of Job, Proverbs and Ecclesiastes. In Mesopotamia perplexity over the moral government of the world was of long standing: to quote W. G. Lambert, 'The problem of the righteous sufferer was certainly implicit from the time of the Third Dynasty of Ur'[1] – and this was a thousand years before Solomon. Poems

[1] *BWL,* p. 10.

on the theme were being written in the days of the patriarchs,[1] and the elaborate works known sometimes as 'The Babylonian Job' (*Ludlul bēl nēmeqi*) and 'The Babylonian Ecclesiastes' (*The Theodicy* – an acrostic dialogue on human misery) were composed, it seems, the former before the days of the Israelite Judges, and the latter probably by the time of David.[2]

Practical wisdom, more akin to that of Proverbs, has an even longer history (its pre-history is interestingly discussed in von Rad's *Old Testament Theology*, I, pp. 418ff.). It may be found embodied in continuous compositions, some of them extremely early (from Egypt *The Teaching of Ptahhotep*, c. 2450 BC, is not the only manual of advice to have preceded Abraham by several centuries), or it may take the form of self-contained sayings. Because the latter have always made excellent copybook material they have survived in large numbers from the writing-exercises of generations of scribes in training.

From Nippur near Babylon, for instance, two big collections of aphorisms written down in the early second millennium BC have been recovered[3] – showing the same mixture of sound morality, dubious morality, sly humour and plain good sense that one meets in the popular sayings of any nation (together with some of the less savoury ingredients of polytheism). For the most part they are observing rather than moralizing: they satirize the boaster or the idler, or the palace officials, or the priest, and crystallize the lessons of experience. On living within one's means, for example:

'Build like a [lord], go about like a slave!
Build like a [sla]ve, go about like a lord!'[4]

Yet they speak sometimes at a deeper level, with equal felicity:

---

[1] *BWL*, pp. 10,11; *WIANE*, pp. 170ff.
[2] *BWL*, pp. 15,67; *DOTT*, p. 97.
[3] *Sumerian Proverbs*, edited by E. I. Gordon (1959); henceforth abbreviated as *SP*.
[4] *SP*, p. 270.

'Whoever has walked with humility – happiness is his store';[1]

and again:

'Whoever has walked with truth generates life.'[2]

This more serious vein reappears in various types of Meso-
potamian literature, from hymns and laments to collections of
precepts, down the centuries. One such collection, *The Words
of Ahikar* (a seventh-century Assyrian sage), which became
virtually world-famous, is of special interest in that it contains
some sayings that have close relatives in Proverbs.[3]

The Egyptian manuals of advice, mentioned above, are
recipes for success in life – some of them specifically for pro-
fessional success. Often the advice is no more than worldly-wise:
here is Ptahhotep on dining with your superior:

'Take what he may give, when it is set before thy nose. . . . Do
not pierce him with many stares. . . . Laugh after he laughs,
and it will be very pleasing to his heart';

and on dealing with a petitioner:

'A petitioner likes attention to his words better than the
fulfilling of that for which he came. . . . a good hearing is a
soothing of the heart.'[4]

This is tact, and tact can be kind or coldblooded. But there
is no ambiguity in the persuasive reminder to a young man, in
The Instruction of Ani, to repay the sacrifices of his mother, and
to foster the self-respect of his wife.

'Thou shouldst not supervise (too closely) thy wife in her

[1] *SP*, p. 41, quoting S. N. Kramer, 'Sumerian Lexical Texts', *AASOR*,
1944.
[2] *SP*, p. 41 (but *cf.* Th. Jacobsen, *ibid.*, p. 448).
[3] See commentary, on 24:17; 25:17; 27:10. As the two latter sayings are
Solomon's, the lender is clearly not Ahikar, a contemporary of Hezekiah.
But the community of interests between this counsellor of Sennacherib and
the men of his enemy Hezekiah as they collected ancient proverbs (see Pr.
25:1) illustrates vividly the international currency of wisdom sayings.
[4] *ANET*, pp. 412,413.

(own) house, when thou knowest that she is efficient. . . . recognize her abilities. How happy it is when thy hand is with her!'[1]

The basic moral precepts are in these writings – warnings against fraud, slander, adultery, *etc.* – and these (as in Proverbs) are presented sometimes as matters of prudence, sometimes as self-authenticating, sometimes as the will of heaven, which abominates the breach of them. Now and then the advice reaches considerable moral heights – occasionally indeed only to disappoint us with a poor motive, but often enough ringing true. It would be hard to better this maxim for a ruler (King Merikare):

'Make thy memorial to last through the love of thee. . . . God will be praised as thy reward';[2]

or this attitude to a bad character, advocated by Amenemope:

'For we shall not act like him –
Lift him up, give him thy hand;
Leave him (in) the hands of the god;
Fill his belly with bread that thou hast,
So that he may be sated and may cast down his eye.'[3]

The general tone of these teachings, though they are mostly more matter-of-fact than this, and also have little to say to the common man, is wholesome and humane: sayings such as the following from Mesopotamia (the *Hymn to Shamash*):

'He who receives no bribe but takes the part of the weak
It is pleasing to Shamash, and he will prolong his life'[4]

or this from Egypt (Ptahhotep again):

'Justice is great, and its appropriateness is lasting . . .'[5]

are more easily found than those that smack of cynicism.

[1] *ANET*, pp. 420,421.
[2] *ANET*, p. 415.
[3] *DOTT*, p. 177.
[4] *DOTT*, p. 109.
[5] *ANET*, p. 412.

Yet when this has been said, the fact remains that an altogether stronger and steadier light burns in Israel. Here there is no distracting plurality of gods and demons, no influence of magic, no cultic licensing of immorality, as in Babylon and Canaan, to muffle the voice of conscience. The details of the Lord's ways in the world may be hidden, and Job and Ecclesiastes must leave our curiosity unsatisfied, but there is ultimate certainty that His way is perfect and His will is sufficiently revealed.[1] So we are spared the paralysing reflection in the 'Babylonian Job':

'I wish I knew that these things were pleasing to one's god!'[2]
(since, for all he could tell, human right was celestial wrong), and spared, too, the wry conclusion of *The Theodicy* that men torment one another because the gods chose to make them that way:

'With lies, and not truth, they endowed them for ever.'[3]

Similarly in the realm of conduct, which is Proverbs' field, the one Lord makes known His will, and thereby a single standard of what is wise and right, and a satisfying motive for seeking it. So a sense of purpose and calling lifts the teaching of Proverbs above the pursuit of success or tranquillity, clear of the confines of a class-ethic or a dry moralism, into the realm of knowing the living God 'in all (one's) ways'.

III. THE STRUCTURE, AUTHORSHIP, DATE AND TEXT OF PROVERBS

The book tells us that it is the work of several authors. Three of these are named (Solomon, Agur and Lemuel), others are mentioned collectively as 'Wise Men', and at least one section of the book (the last) is anonymous. There is one editorial note (25:1) to say when one of the sections was compiled, but

---

[1] *Cf.* Dt. 29:29; Pr. 30:5,6.
[2] *Ludlul*, 33 (*cf.* 34ff.); *BWL*, p. 41.
[3] *DOTT*, p. 102.

nothing is said of the date at which the collections were all brought together.

a. The structure and authorship

The sections are as follows:

Title, Introduction and Motto: 1:1–7
I. A Father's Praise of Wisdom: 1:8 – 9:18
II. Proverbs of Solomon: 10:1 – 22:16
IIIa. Words of Wise Men: 22:17 – 24:22
IIIb. Further Words of Wise Men: 24:23–34
IV. Further Proverbs of Solomon (Hezekiah's Collection): 25:1 – 29:27
V. Words of Agur: 30:1–33
VI. Words of King Lemuel: 31:1–9
VII. An Alphabet of Wifely Excellence: 31:10–31

The title (1:1), 'The proverbs of Solomon', may be intended as a section-heading to chapters 1–9 or as the editor's title of the whole book. I take it to be the latter.[1] On the present view, Solomon is named at the outset as the principal author, although his own collection of proverbs will not be reached till chapter 10, where the heading is repeated. (If chapters 1–9 consisted of proverbs of Solomon we should expect 10:1 to be phrased: 'These also are proverbs of Solomon', on the pattern of 24:23 and 25:1.)

Solomon's own proverbs are deferred for the good reason that the reader needs preparation if he is to use them fruitfully. So the *introduction* (1:2–6), an extension of the title, makes it clear that this book is no anthology, but a course of education in the life of wisdom. The *motto* (1:7) at once goes to the heart of the matter, and *Section I* (1:8 – 9:18) expounds it in a series of fatherly talks which illustrate and press home to the pupil the fateful choice he must make between wisdom and folly. By now the reader is in a position to orientate himself in the thicket

---

[1] For another opinion see E. J. Young, *Introduction to the Old Testament* (1964 edn.), p. 311.

of individual sayings which he enters in *Section II* (10:1 – 22:16), and to see in each cool, objective aphorism a miniature and particular outworking of the wisdom and folly whose whole course he has seen spread out before him in Section I.

In *Section III* (*a*. 22:17 – 24:22; *b*. 24:23–24) the teaching style returns – less expansively than in chapters 1–9, but none-theless in sayings that spread into paragraphs and speak directly to the reader. There is a hand on our shoulder again.

Scholars have debated since 1923 the relation of this section to the Egyptian *Teaching of Amenemope*, which was published in that year by Wallis Budge. As the references in the commentary will show, the points of contact between the two are too many and too close to be a matter of coincidence. Almost the whole of Proverbs 22:17 – 23:14 (which constitutes a subsection of IIIa, as the fresh start in verse 15 suggests) is closely paralleled in widely-scattered sayings in *Amenemope*. (The exceptions are 22:23,26,27; 23:13,14.) After this concentration there is one more parallel in Section III, at 24:29, and in the rest of Proverbs a sprinkling of about seven, confined to the two Solomonic collections (12:22; 15:16,17; 16:11; 20:23; 25:21; 26:9; 27:1).

The fact that Amenemope in these shared sayings sometimes rises to heights that are worthier of an Israelite and a Christian than of a polytheist and a seeker of tranquillity, creates an initial presumption that he is the borrower. Close scrutiny of the wording and contexts of the parallels, however, has led almost all scholars to the opposite conclusion, since it is the Hebrew text that tends to be clarified when it is read by the side of its longer Egyptian counterpart. (For a striking example, solving an old problem of translation, see the commentary at 22:20.) While some scholars in their enthusiasm have over-stated the case, and trimmed the Hebrew needlessly to the shape of the Egyptian[1] – forgetting the freedom of the Hebrew

---

[1] *E.g.* in D. C. Simpson's collation (*JEA*, 1926, pp. 232 ff.) nearly half his parallels introduce emendations; and J. Gray clings to an Amenemope-based reading of 23: 4 while admitting that it is now lexicographically un-necessary (*The Legacy of Canaan*, 1957, p. 195).

author – it still remains a good case. E. Drioton re-opened the question in 1957 and 1959[1] by arguing from numerous examples that the Egyptian was a mere translation from a Hebrew original; but he did not consider that Proverbs was that original, only a joint borrower; and in any case his linguistic arguments seem to be effectively refuted by R. J. Williams, who has produced Egyptian counterparts of all the alleged Semitisms.[2]

The contention that Proverbs has made use of Amenemope (and not *vice versa*) has now been greatly strengthened, if not clinched, by chronological evidence. An ostracon in the Cairo Museum containing an extract from the *Teaching* seems to show that Amenemope must be dated well before the time of Solomon: W. F. Albright suggests the twelfth century,[3] and J. M. Plumley *c.* 1300 BC.[4] In Israelite terms these dates mean the days of the Judges or of Moses, and no-one has yet suggested that Solomon was writing then! (On the question whether or not Israel was likely to use raw material from abroad, it may be pointed out that the title, 'Words of Wise Men', implies or at least accords with some diversity of sources, and that Sections V and VI are both by foreigners; see also the account of Wisdom in the Ancient World, pp. 17ff.) But if Proverbs is the borrower here, the borrowing is not slavish but free and creative. Egyptian jewels, as at the Exodus, have been re-set to their advantage by Israelite workmen and put to finer use.

Section IV (chapters 25–29) has Solomon's own touch in its terse sayings, as in Section II. But Hezekiah's scribes have introduced more grouping of sayings than the earlier section can show (*e.g.* kings and courtiers, 25:2–7 (but *cf.* 16:10–15); fools, 26:1,3–12; sluggards, 26:13–16; mischief-makers, 26:17–28); they have also used some longer sayings, and (except in chapter 28) fewer antitheses.

Sections V (chapter 30) *and VI* (31:1–9) are both from non-Israelites, perhaps Arabians from Massa (see commentary).

---

[1] *Mélanges Bibliques,* 1957, pp. 254ff.; *Sacra Pagina,* 1959, pp. 229ff.
[2] *JEA,* 1961, pp. 100ff.
[3] *WIANE,* p. 13.
[4] *DOTT,* p. 173.

The language of 30:4 and the spelling of the word for God in 30:5 are reminiscent of the book of Job, which is set in the same region. We know nothing of these two authors. In the LXX these sections are displaced (showing perhaps that they once circulated independently[1]), to straddle the 'Further Words of Wise Men' in 24:23ff. and to swell chapter 24 to 77 verses.

Section VII (31:10–31), an alphabetic acrostic, is anonymous: in the LXX it is separated from the previous section by five chapters (see note above). Its portrait of a fine wife brings this book of wholesome living to a fitting close, showing a united family (31:28ff.) honouring the one who, under God, can do most to build up the character extolled in these pages.

b. *The date*

Until about the mid-point of this century, critical opinion was largely agreed that the Sages came rather late on the Israelite scene, to produce the bulk of their work after the Exile. It was conceded that Proverbs contained some pre-exilic matter, but the mature conception of wisdom in chapters 1–9 seemed to owe too much to Persian[2] or Greek[3] thought to have taken shape before the fifth to third centuries BC; and this line of argument was reinforced by Gunkel's theory of the internal development of wisdom teaching, whereby the briefer a unit was, the earlier it must be; and the longer and more spiritual, the later.

However, a growing knowledge of Egyptian and Babylonian teachings from the millennium before Solomon, and of Phoenician literature from fourteenth century Ugarit (Ras Shamra) has made it clear that the *content* of Proverbs (whatever the date of its editing) is at home in the world of early Israel rather than post-exilic Judaism, in its thought, vocabulary, style and, often, its metric forms. The idea that the wisdom movement in Israel belonged to the late Persian and early Greek period is seen now to have been 'a curious myth' of our

---

[1] See, for a different theory, C. C. Torrey, *JBL*, 1954, pp. 93ff.

[2] O. S. Rankin, *Israel's Wisdom Literature* (1936), p. 252.

[3] C. H. Toy, *Proverbs* (*ICC*), p. xxii.

times, and Gunkel's form-criterion (which is belied by these early literatures) a 'strait jacket' too long endured.[1] The most far-reaching element in this general reassessment is the realization that chapters 8 and 9 (hitherto considered the latest part of the book) are closest of all to Israel's early Canaanite background, and conceivably as early as Solomon. When we add the probability that Amenemope is to be dated in or before the days of the Judges (see above, p. 24), it emerges that the content of the two major undated collections in Proverbs (chapters 1–9 and 22:17 – 24:33), which incidentally contain some of the boldest doctrinal and ethical material in the book, shows most clearly the influence of early sources. The two Solomonic collections (10:1 – 22:16, and chapters 25–29) announce their own dates, and we are left with only chapters 30–31 to consider. Of these, nothing certain can be said. It may be worth pointing out however that the nature-sayings of chapter 30 are examples of a subject that especially attracted Solomon (1 Ki. 4:33). 31:1–9 gives no clue of its date; 31:10–31 is equally indeterminate: its acrostic form might be early or late (the Babylonian *Theodicy* of *c.* 1000 BC is a very elaborate acrostic), and the glimpse of Abigail in 1 Samuel 25 is a reminder that there were great ladies in the land even in the days of Saul, 'who clothed (them) in scarlet...' (2 Sa. 1:24; Pr. 31:21).

As to its *editing*, Proverbs gives us one statement (25:1), which shows that the book was still in the making at *c.* 700 BC, about 250 years after Solomon. It is a fair assumption, but no more, that chapters 30–31 were added later as existing collections, and chapters 1–9 placed as the introduction to the whole by the final editor (see above, Structure and Authorship, pp. 22ff.). Whether 1–9 itself has a history of growth is an open question: the only tangible clues are on the one hand the evident antiquity of (especially) chapters 8 and 9, already discussed, and on the other hand the occurrence of a probably Greek-based word for 'linen' (RSV) in 7:16. The latter could imply that the book was still growing in the Greek period (*i.e.* 330 BC onwards); but it need not, for such names travelled with trade. Other arguments

[1] W. F. Albright, in *WIANE*, p. 4.

are equally inconclusive; *e.g.* the fatherly style of these chapters can be matched either with Ben Sira (*c.* 180 BC) or with Amene-mope, a thousand years before him. Whether the book reached completion in Hezekiah's reign, or not until a century or so before Ben Sira, who used it, we cannot tell; all that can be said is that its contents could all have been in existence, though not all gathered into one book (see again 25:1) in Solomon's life-time.

c. The text

A reader of Proverbs in the RSV will find on most pages a number of notes of 'corrections' and of preferred readings from 'Gk Syr Vg and Tg', *i.e.* from the Greek 'Septuagint' translation (often known as LXX) begun in the third century BC, the Syriac 'Peshitta' (dependent on the Hebrew text and the LXX) begun in the first century AD, the Latin 'Vulgate' translated by Jerome in the fourth century AD from the Hebrew (but with the help of existing Greek and Latin translations), and finally the Targums, which were Aramaic translations (some of them very free) from the Hebrew, for use in the synagogues, in oral form at first, but put into writing from about the fifth century AD. The Targum on Proverbs is among the stricter translations.

The frequent recourse to these versions may give the impres-sion that the Hebrew Text (known as the MT, *i.e.* the Massoretic Text) is in bad shape in Proverbs; but this is not so. Here and there we meet a phrase that seems so ungrammatical or inappropriate that a copyist's error has to be assumed, and the versions invoked; but it happens rather seldom. Just how seldom must be a matter of opinion; and three things may be pointed out about this:

1. Our understanding of Hebrew is incomplete. A growing knowledge of related languages and literatures has already thrown light on many words which had been the despair of translators (see, *e.g.*, note on 26:23), and should encourage us to treat a hard text more often as awaiting explanation than as needing correction.

2. The ancient versions are imperfect. These versions, especially the LXX, provide a valuable window on the Hebrew text that lay before their translators in ancient times; but the window has its own peculiarities. It may be unduly severe to say that 'The Septuagint belongs more to the history of Old Testament exegesis than to that of the Old Testament text',[1] but it is salutary to remember that its version of Proverbs is among the 'free, sometimes paraphrasing translations',[2] that it adds many sayings of its own and makes various omissions, and, as G. Gerleman has shown,[3] tends to adapt the style and content of the original to the somewhat Hellenized outlook of the translator. When the LXX therefore provides a more shapely antithesis or a less violent simile than the Hebrew, it may well be offering only a judicious re-touching, not a purer text.

3. Our canons of style are not the authors'. Modern hands itch to smooth away irregularities – often overlooking the fact that an asymmetrical proverb can be richer than a symmetrical, by containing both an implied antithesis and a stated one (see note on 15:2). The love of logical tidiness is a modern, western trait, like the distaste for mixed metaphors; it is a poor guide to knowing what a Hebrew author wrote at a given point.

In this commentary therefore the Hebrew text is given the benefit of the doubt, wherever it yields a tolerable sense. It should perhaps be added that this text consisted only of consonants, the vowels being remembered by tradition while Hebrew was a living language, and signs for them eventually placed above and below the consonants. So the consonantal text is our written link with the authors, and in spite of the tenacity of the Jewish memory of the vowels, we can assume a little more likelihood of mistakes of pronunciation (and so of meaning) creeping in, than of consonantal changes. Where a

---

[1] G. Bertram, quoted by E. Würthwein, *The Text of the Old Testament* (1957), p. 50.
[2] H. St. J. Thackeray, *Grammar of Old Testament Greek according to the LXX* (1909), I, p. 13 (quoted by G. Gerleman, 'The LXX Proverbs as a Hellenistic Document', in *OTS*, VIII, pp. 15ff.).
[3] *Ibid.*

change of vowels, then, seems required, we are readier to resort to it than to a change of consonants; but we have tried to play as little as possible the alluring guessing-game of conjectural emendation.

SUBJECT-STUDIES

GOD AND MAN[1]

When we open the book of Proverbs at random and take samples
of its wisdom, we may gain the impression that its religious
content is thin and indefinite. Many of its maxims and theological assertions would transplant into non-Israelite, non-
biblical soil,[2] and we are tempted to ask whether anything as
specific as a covenant-relationship with God is presupposed
here. A hostile reader might go even further, and ask whether
the real God and master in this book is not man himself, and the
real goal prosperity.

Although this last question can be answered quickly, it is
not enough to point to the recurrent motto: 'The fear of the
Lord is the beginning of wisdom' (9:10 and parallels); for
this could be itself a mere counsel of prudence, a crowning
example of a policy of cultivating the powers that be. The
answer is seen rather in the relation of prudential considerations
to moral, throughout the book; and it is a clear answer. The
moral factors always take precedence. To be sure, Proverbs
is concerned to point out that what is right and what pays may
travel long distances together; but it leaves us in no doubt which
we are to follow when their paths diverge. *E.g.*, on the question of
gifts and bribes, it will go as far as to say, without demur, 'A
man's gift (*mattān*) maketh room for him, and bringeth him
before great men' (18:16); but it will not go a step further.
'A wicked man', says 17:23, 'taketh a bribe (*šōḥaḏ*) out of the
bosom, to pervert the ways of justice' – and it is at once clear that
justice, not success, is our proper concern, and that the unscrupulous will get no praise for their fancied wisdom. You

[1] A revision and abbreviation of an article in *The Tyndale House Bulletin*,
July 1961.
[2] See pp. 25f.

have to be good to be wise – though Proverbs is particularly concerned to point out the converse: that you have to be wise to be really good; for goodness and wisdom are not two separable qualities, but two aspects of a single whole. To take it further back, you have to be *godly* to be wise; and this is not because godliness pays, but because the only wisdom by which you can handle everyday things in conformity with their nature is the wisdom by which they were divinely made and ordered. Proverbs 8, which states this superlatively, is therefore far from being a non-functional pinnacle of the book's eloquence, but is rather an exposure of the main framework of its thought.

That God is a reality to these writers is confirmed by their sense of sin – a shadow only thrown by some sense of the divine. 'Who can say, I have made my heart clean, I am pure from my sin?' (20:9). In Proverbs this is not the servile uneasiness that the Gentile felt ('God, known or unknown – my transgressions are many. . . . The transgression I have committed – I know not. . . . Whether one does wrong or right one knows not'[1]); if the service of God is exacting, it is for the opposite reason, that His servants are counted as men who know His will and should share His zeal. 'Rescue those who are . . . stumbling to the slaughter. If you say, "Behold, we did not know this," does not he who weighs the heart perceive it? . . . and will he not requite man according to his work?' (24:11,12, RSV). No evasions are countenanced; religious exercises will buy no favours: 'He that turneth away his ear from hearing the law, even his prayer is an abomination' (28:9), and so is his sacrifice (15:8; 21:27). Sin must be put away in practical repentance ('by mercy and truth . . . and by the fear of the Lord', 16:6) and in frank confession ('whoso confesseth and forsaketh them shall obtain mercy', 28:13). In a word, there are no subpersonal transactions.

So far, it is clear that God is no afterthought here, and goodness no poor relation to cleverness. But are we left with nothing stronger than moralistic theism?

An indication of the answer appears as soon as the sayings

[1] A Sumerian *Prayer to any God*, ll.24,26,53; *DOTT*, pp. 113–114.

which mention God are searched out. Of about 100 such proverbs, all but a dozen use the covenant name Yahweh. As far as terminology goes, then, the book belongs to the covenant people, and God is the God who revealed His name to Moses. If we can also find indications that between Him and man there is a stable relationship assumed – on man's side filial, and on God's side faithful and self-revealing – we shall have found as much evidence of the covenant as a collection of proverbs can be expected to yield.

We may start with the motto, and ask whether the 'fear' of the Lord implies anything more than a healthy respect for the Almighty. This it clearly does. In two passages, 2:5 and 9:10, it is made synonymous with the *knowledge* of Him; and this knowledge is remarkably intimate. It is given by revelation ('out of his mouth', 2:6) and fostered by what could be called the practice of His presence, as commended in 3:6: 'In all thy ways acknowledge him', or literally, '*know* him'. We are reminded of the goal of the new covenant itself ('they shall all know me'), for 'the upright are in his confidence' (3:32), *i.e.* His *sōd̲*, His intimate circle.

Such intercourse 'in all thy ways' implies, in addition to reverence and obedience, *trust*; and it is noteworthy that Proverbs, for all its emphasis on common sense, exalts faith above sagacity (3:5,7: 'Trust in the Lord with all thine heart; and upon thine own understanding lean not; ... Be not wise in thine own eyes ...'); and for all its advocacy of prudence it refuses prudence the last word. Planning, proper as it is ('Plans are established by counsel: by wise guidance wage war', 20:18) – planning is subject to *God's* Yes or No (19:21: 'Many are the plans in the mind of a man, but it is the purpose of Yahweh that will be established'); equipment guarantees nothing (21:31: 'The horse is prepared against the day of battle: but safety is of the Lord'); and caution can be fatal in a way that faith cannot ('The fear of man bringeth a snare; but they that trust in Yahweh shall be safe', 29:25). Such teaching is virtually that of Isaiah in his dealings with those who looked to Assyria or to the horses of Egypt for help; indeed, one writer can declare specifically that the object of his maxims is to foster, not self-reliance, but faith: 'That thy trust may be in the Lord, I have made them known to thee' (22:19).

This faith is not regarded as a last resort or a useful habit of mind: it can be traced, here and there in Proverbs, down to its roots in a steady relationship of exactly the kind which the covenant established. There is admittedly only one mention of covenant in the book, and even this shows the human participant in an all too characteristic position: 'the adventuress . . . who forsakes the companion of her youth and forgets the covenant of her God' (2:16,17). But whether this means the Sinai covenant or not (see commentary), God is referred to as '*her* God', and it is this that makes her sin specially heinous. The same personal bond with God is prominent in Agur's thoughts in 30:7–9, for his fear is not so much of isolated sins (though he does abhor them) as of a breach of loyalty: 'lest I deny thee' – for the Lord is not simply 'God' to him, but '*my* God'. This is the essence of covenant language. The quintessence is found in the statement of father-and-son relationship in 3:12: 'Whom the Lord loveth he reproveth; even as a father the son in whom he delighteth'.

There is still a final question. Granted that in Proverbs the covenant relationship is assumed, is it a purely private bond which has no place for the institutions of Israelite religion? Undoubtedly man is not seen in these chapters as Israelite man first and foremost, as he tends to be seen elsewhere in the Old Testament. But the institutions are assumed, even if they are not stressed. There is prayer and sacrifice, although the emphasis about their use is that of the Prophets: 'To do justice and judgment is more acceptable to the Lord than sacrifice' (21:3). There is also revelation. While Proverbs normally presents the wise man's own teaching or *tôrâ* to the pupil as '*my tôrâ*', there looms behind it '*the tôrâ*', majestic and absolute. It is only moral perversity that can reject it: 'Those who forsake the law praise the wicked' (28:4). As for a people deprived of revelation, 29:18 holds out little hope for them. 'Where there is no vision' (or, RSV, 'prophecy') 'the people run wild; but he that keepeth the law' (the other main form of Old Testament revelation), 'happy is he'.

To end on this note, however, would be to disguise the fact that the explicitly religious material has to be hand-picked from a large mass of sayings in which religion is only implicit. And we should do Proverbs a poor service if we contrived to vest it in a priestly ephod or a prophet's mantle, for it is a book which seldom takes you to church. Like its own figure of Wisdom, it calls across to you in the street about some everyday matter, or points things out at home. Its function in Scripture is to put godliness into working clothes; to name business and society as spheres in which we are to acquit ourselves with credit to our Lord, and in which we are to look for His training.

If we could analyse the influences that build up a godly character to maturity, we might well find that the agencies which we call natural vastly outweighed those that we call supernatural. The book of Proverbs reassures us that this, if it is true, is no reflection on the efficiency of God's grace; for the hard facts of life, which knock some of the nonsense out of us, are *God's* facts and His appointed school of character; they are not alternatives to His grace, but means of it; for everything *is* of grace, from the power to know to the power to obey. 'The hearing ear and the seeing eye, the Lord has made them both' (20:12).

Yet while all go to God's school, few learn wisdom there, for the knowledge which He aims to instil is the knowledge of Himself; and this, too, is the ultimate prize. In submission to His authority and majesty (that is, in the fear of the Lord) we alone start and continue our education; and by the diligent search for wisdom 'as for hid treasures' we shall find our prize in a growing intimacy with the same Lord. He is the beginning; He is also the end; for the goal is: 'Then shalt thou understand the fear of the Lord, and find the knowledge of God' (2:5).

WISDOM

I. THE MANY FACETS OF WISDOM

The book of Proverbs opens by breaking up the plain daylight of wisdom (*ḥokmâ*) into its rainbow of constituent colours. These all shade into one another, and any one of them can be used to represent the whole; yet there is some value in seeing them momentarily analysed and grouped.

1. *Instruction*, or *training* (*mûsār*; 1:2a,3a), a far from static term, is the first synonym, giving notice at once that wisdom will be hard-won, a quality of character as much as of mind. This word has usually (not invariably – see *e.g.* 4:1) a note of sternness, ranging from warning (*e.g.* 24:32) to chastening (whether by the Lord, 3:11, or by the rod, 23:13; *cf.* the extreme instance: Is. 53:5). Its frequent companion is *correction*, or *reproof* (*tôkaḥat*; 1:23; 3:11, *etc.*), a noun whose derivation emphasizes verbal rather than physical persuasion: an appeal to reason and conscience (*cf.* Is. 1:18; *cf.* Jn. 16:8 with the LXX's equivalent of *tôkaḥat*). The two terms together can be summed up as *discipline*; they give the reminder that wisdom is not to be had through extra-mural study: it is for disciples only.

2. The second synonym in Proverbs 1 is *understanding*, or *insight* (*bînâ*, 1:2b; *tᵉḇûnâ*, 2:2, *etc.*). The background idea (though it is not always prominent) can be gauged from the fact that the verb 'to discern' is parent to both nouns, and the preposition 'between' is a near relation. Solomon put the two together in 1 Kings 3:9: 'that I may *discern between* good and evil'. (*Cf.* Phil. 1:9,10; Heb. 5:14.) Another word (*lēḇ*, 'heart', *i.e.* 'mind') is also rendered 'understanding' in AV and RV, but is better called *sense*, as in RSV: *e.g.* 6:32; 10:13; *cf.* Ho. 7:11.

3. The third is *wise dealing* (derivatives of the root *ś-k-l*: *haśkēl*, 1:3a; *maśkîl*, 10:5; *śekel*, 12:8), *i.e.* good sense, practical wisdom, *savoir-faire*. Its particular character shows in its verb-form, which often means 'be successful'. Eve, in the

garden, misconceived it as sophistication (Gn. 3:6), but Abigail finely displayed it in her handling of a crisis (1 Sa. 25:3). Its supreme expression (giving the lie to Eve) is in the unworldly triumph of the Servant of the Lord: Isaiah 52:13. At its first appearance in Proverbs it is claimed for the right master by being coupled with 'righteousness, judgment and equity' (1:3b). A companion term is *tûšiyyâ* (*e.g.* 2:7a; 8:14; Is. 28:29c), *sound wisdom*.

4. In the same range lie the expressions *shrewdness* ('*ormâ*, 1:4a) and *discretion* (*mᵉzimmâ*, 1:4b) – the former of these seen in enemy hands in Genesis 3:1, and the latter (which means, in C. H. Toy's words, 'the power of forming plans') so often degenerating into mere scheming that it can be used by itself in a bad sense (*e.g.* 12:2) more often than in a good. But these qualities need not be corrupt, and the book is largely concerned to show that the godly man is in the best sense a man of affairs, who takes the trouble to know his way about, and plan his course realistically (*cf.* 22:3: 'a shrewd man sees danger and hides himself; but the simple go on, and suffer for it'). To use the literal meaning of *counsels* (*tahbūlôt*, 1:5), he knows *the ropes*.

5. A fifth group consists of the words *knowledge* (*daʿaṭ*) and *learning* (*leqaḥ*, 1:5)[1]; the former implying not so much an informed mind as a knowing of truth and indeed of God Himself (2:5; 3:6), and the latter tending to emphasize that doctrine is something given and received, or grasped.

II. THE ATTAINMENT OF WISDOM

Wisdom is for anyone who wants it. Fools and simpletons are invited by name to its feast, which is as free as that of folly (9:4, 16).

At the same time, it is as costly as character. Its largesse is

---

[1] The word *leqaḥ* is derived from the verb 'to take'; hence it can also mean in some contexts 'persuasiveness', as in 7:21a; 16:21,23; *cf.* our expression: 'very taking'. The writer was encouraged to find that D. W. Thomas makes a similar comparison (*WIANE*, p. 284).

not scattered, but 'stored up' for the 'upright', for men of 'integrity', for 'saints' (2:7–9).

To put the antithesis differently: wisdom comes by *revelation* ('For it is the Lord who gives wisdom: from his mouth come knowledge and understanding' (2:6); 'Add not thou to his words' (30:6)); it also comes by *discipleship*; the verse 2:6, just quoted, follows a call to strenuous search in 2:1–5, 'as for hid treasures' (4), which is a search for God Himself (5). The demands that it makes may be summarized as follows.

1. *Conversion*: a *turning from* evil – for 'the fear of the Lord' (which is the beginning of wisdom, 9:10) 'is to hate evil' (8:13; *cf*. 3:7b) – and from one's cherished independence, that way that 'seems right to a man' (14:12); positively, a *turning to* the light; indeed to God's salvation. 'Turn in hither', says wisdom (9:4); and the range of her invitation anticipates the gospel offer: 'Come . . . eat . . . drink . . . forsake . . . live . . . walk' (9:5, 6).

2. *Devotion*. Wisdom is for the humbly eager – one might almost say, for the lover, the suitor '. . . watching daily at my gates, waiting at the posts of my doors' (8:34). It is not for the man 'wise in his own eyes': he thinks he has arrived – and indeed he has, for he will never get a step further. His trouble is not intellectual; he is no fool: 'there is more hope of a fool than of him' (26:12; *cf*. 3:7). It is that he does not seriously want to be a better person; whereas the wise man is teachable to the end (9:9), open to God's commands (10:8) and chastening (3:11ff.; see also above, 1 (1)), and to human advice and criticism (13:10; 17:10); for he values truth enough to pay the price of having it (23:23).

III. THE PRE-EMINENCE OF WISDOM

Since chapter 8 is entirely devoted to this theme, it is enough to call attention to it, and to the comments there.

THE FOOL

The fool meets us under various names. It will be convenient to treat these separately, but some of the terms (especially in section II) are virtually interchangeable.

I. THE SIMPLE

The Hebrew word is *peṭî*. The verb formed from this word (like our verb 'to fool') means to deceive or seduce (as in 1:10: 'if sinners entice thee'), and the *peṭî*, accordingly, is the kind of person who is easily led, gullible, silly. Mentally, he is naïve ('the simple believes everything, but the prudent looks where he is going', 14:15; *cf.* 22:3); morally, he is wilful and irresponsible ('the waywardness of the simple shall slay them', 1:32).

Because of his lazy thoughtlessness, he may need a visual aid to bring him to repentance ('Smite a scorner, and the simple will learn sense', 19:25). If he refuses it, he will graduate to a more serious condition: 'The simple acquire folly' (*'iwwelet* – see II(2), below), 'but the prudent are crowned with knowledge' (14:18); for one does not stay still: a man who is emptyheaded will end up wrongheaded. In fact to the truly emptyheaded, those whom Proverbs calls *ḥªsar-lēḇ*, senseless, folly is 'fun' (15:21), for they have nothing better to do than 'chase after vanities' (12:11).

The *locus classicus* of the 'simple' is chapter 7, where he is seen at his most typical: aimless, inexperienced, drifting into temptation – indeed almost courting it. A person in such a state (and the reader is not encouraged to think himself beyond such folly) will not go far before he meets a temptress, or (as in 1:10ff.) tempters, who know what they want and what he half wants. In short, the simple (and his elder brother, the fool) is no halfwit; he is a person whose instability could be rectified, but who prefers not to accept discipline in the school of wisdom (1:22–32).

II. THE FOOL

In Proverbs, three words are translated 'fool'.

1. *kᵉsîl*. This is the commonest of the three terms, occurring nearly 50 times. By derivation, it seems to mean one who is dull and obstinate; but it must always be remembered that the book has in mind a man's chosen outlook, rather than his mental equipment. We are shown the *kᵉsîl* as he is first in himself, and second in society.

In himself, he has no idea of a patient search for wisdom: he has not the concentration for it ('a fool's eyes are in the ends of the earth', 17:24), but imagines it can be handed out to him over the counter ('Why does a fool offer the sage a fee, when he has no mind to learn?' 17:16, Moffatt). So he 'laps up' his opinions unreflectingly (see note on 15:14), and pours them out freely (15:2), unaware that he is only displaying his folly as a trader spreads out his goods (13:16). His sage remarks either fall flat or turn round on him (26:7, 9); but he will never realize this, for he cannot imagine himself mistaken. 'A rebuke enters deeper into a discerning man than a hundred stripes into a fool' (17:10).

The root of his trouble is spiritual, not mental. He *likes* his folly, going back to it 'like a dog that returns to his vomit' (26:11); he has no reverence for truth, preferring comfortable illusions (see 14:8, and note). At bottom, what he is rejecting is the fear of the Lord (1:29): it is this that constitutes him a fool, and this that makes his complacency tragic; for 'the careless ease of fools shall destroy them' (1:32).

In society the fool is, in a word, a menace. At best, he wastes your time: 'you will not find a word of sense in him' (14:7, Moffatt); and he may be a more serious nuisance. If he has an idea in his head, nothing will stop him: 'let a bear robbed of her whelps meet a man, rather than a fool in his folly' (17:12) – whether that folly is some prank that is beyond a joke (10:23), or some quarrel he must pick (18:6) and run to death (29:11). Give him a wide berth, for 'the companion of fools shall smart for it' (13:20), and if you want to send him away, don't send him with a message (26:6)!

Some people, however, cannot disown him; it is their tragedy. To his father and mother the fool brings sorrow (10:1; 17:21), bitterness (17:25) and calamity (19:13). It is the price of loving him; but it causes him no qualms – he despises them (15:20).

2. *'ĕwîl* (19 times). Like *kᵉsîl* above, this word suggests stupidity and stubbornness; and the fact that the 'folly' of the *kᵉsîl* is almost always called *'iwwelet* (from the same root as *'ĕwîl*) shows that these two names for 'fool' are virtually one. Yet the present term is, if anything, a darker one than *kᵉsîl*, as used in Proverbs.

The fool, by this name as by the other, gives himself away as soon as he opens his mouth (17:28; 24:7; *cf.* 10:14), and he is as quarrelsome as his other self – for he knows no restraint (20:3; 12:16) and has no sense of proportion (27:3; 29:9). The feature that seems specially prominent is his *moral insolence*: from his first appearance onwards he is impatient of all advice (1:7; 10:8; 12:15; 15:5), and his flippant outlook is crystallized in the famous phrase, 'fools make a mock at sin' (14:9). It is small wonder that his folly – unless it is knocked out of him early (22:15) – is virtually ineradicable. 'Though thou shouldest bray a fool in a mortar . . . with a pestle, yet will not his foolishness depart from him' (27:22).

3. *nābāl*. This word occurs only three times in Proverbs (its verb, 30:32, appears once), and adds little to the picture already built up, except an extra weight of boorishness (17:7, where see note; 30:22). It does underline, however, the fact that the fool, by whatever name he goes, is by definition one whose mind is closed, for the present at least, to God (like the *nābāl* of Ps. 14:1) and to reason (like the Nabal of whom his wife said 'One cannot speak to him', 1 Sa. 25:17), since he has rejected the first principle of wisdom, the fear of the Lord.

III. THE SCOFFER

The scoffer or scorner (*lēṣ*) makes about seventeen appearances in the book, and is contrasted with the wise, or coupled with the foolish, often enough to earn a place of his own in the fools' gallery. His presence there makes it finally clear that mental attitude, not mental capacity, classifies the man. He shares with his fellows their strong dislike of correction (9:7,8; 13:1; 15:12), and it is this, not any lack of intelligence, that blocks any move he makes towards wisdom (14:6). The mischief he does is not the random mischief of the ordinary fool, but the deeper damage of the 'debunker' and deliberate trouble-maker (21:24; 22:10; 29:8). He impresses the impressionable, as long as he is allowed his way (19:25; 21:11); but his bad influence is plain to most men (24:9). Of the 'judgments . . . prepared for scorners' (19:29), the final and most withering is a deep draught of their own medicine: 'He (the Lord) scorneth the scorners' (3:34).

THE SLUGGARD

I. THE SLUGGARD'S CHARACTER

The sluggard in Proverbs is a figure of tragi-comedy, with his sheer animal laziness (he is more than anchored to his bed: he is *hinged* to it, 26:14), his preposterous excuses ('there is a lion outside!' 26:13; 22:13) and his final helplessness.

1. *He will not begin things.* When we ask him (6:9,10) 'How long . . . ?' 'When . . . ?', we are being too definite for him. He doesn't know. All he knows is his delicious drowsiness; all he asks is a little respite: 'a little . . . a little . . . a little . . .'. He does not commit himself to a refusal, but deceives himself by the smallness of his surrenders. So, by inches and minutes, his opportunity slips away.

2. *He will not finish things.* The rare effort of beginning has been too much; the impulse dies. So his quarry goes bad on him (12:27, AV, RV; see commentary) and his meal goes cold on him (19:24; 26:15).

3. *He will not face things.* He comes to believe his own excuses (perhaps there *is* a lion out there, 22:13), and to rationalize his laziness; for he is 'wiser in his own conceit than seven men that can render a reason' (26:16). Because he makes a habit

of the soft choice (he 'will not plow by reason of the cold', 20:4, AV – see commentary) his character suffers as much as his business, so that he is implied in 15:19 (see commentary) to be fundamentally dishonest. (A suggestion of the way he would describe himself is made in the commentary on 26:13–16.)

4. Consequently he is *restless* (13:4; 21:25,26) with unsatisfied desire; *helpless* in face of the tangle of his affairs, which are like a 'hedge of thorns' (15:19); and *useless* – expensively (18:9) and exasperatingly (10:26) – to any who must employ him.

II. THE SLUGGARD'S LESSON

1. *By example.* The *locus classicus* is 6:6ff.: 'Go to the ant . . .' – for she shames the sluggard twice over. First, in needing no 'overseer' (7), whereas *he* must be prodded; he waits for it, resigned and defensive. Secondly, in 'knowing the time'. To him, all time is alike: summer and harvest (8) suggest long, languorous days (*cf.* 10:5), rather than the time of crisis in which the year's work will be crowned or cancelled, and the battle with winter decided (*cf.* Je. 8:20). Like the pharaoh of Jeremiah 46:17, 'he hath let the appointed time pass by'; like the slumbering watchmen of Isaiah 56:9–12, his motto is 'tomorrow shall be as to-day was, and braver, braver yet!' (Knox's translation).

2. *By experience.* This lesson comes too late. He will suddenly wake to find that poverty has *arrived* ('like a vagabond, . . . like an armed man', 6:11, RSV), and there is no arguing with it. Through shirking hard work he has qualified for drudgery (just when his too energetic friend has risen to more rewarding duties, 12:24); and through procrastination the disorder of his life has become irreversible: all is wasteland (24:30,31).

'Then I beheld, and considered well: I saw, and received instruction' (24:32). The wise man will learn while there is time. He knows that the sluggard is no freak, but, as often as not, an ordinary man who has made too many excuses, too many refusals and too many postponements. It has all been as imperceptible, and as pleasant, as falling asleep.

THE FRIEND

I. FRIENDS AND NEIGHBOURS

The common word for 'friend' (*rēa'*) means, equally, 'neigh-bour': it has very much the range of meaning of our word 'fellow'. At the far extreme, it signifies merely 'the other fellow'; at its nearest it stands for a person with whom one has close fellowship. The context will decide the point. At one moment one's *rēa'* is an opponent at law (18:17); at another he is the one who 'loveth at all times' (17:17). The use of the term in Leviticus 19:18 ('thou shalt love thy *rēa'* as thyself') suggests that God means us to reverse the depersonalizing process which the word's use reflects. (Even the stronger word, *'ohēḇ*, 'one who loves', can be debased from its high status of, *e.g.*, 18:24b and 27:6, to denoting the sycophants of 14:20.)

On the other hand, Proverbs itself is emphatic that a few close friends are better than a host of acquaintances, and stand in a class by themselves. (Our Lord's relationship with the 'beloved disciple' endorses the point.) Therefore we shall consider first the good neighbour, and secondly the good friend.

a. The good neighbour

The neighbourly qualities which Proverbs urges on the reader add up to nothing less than love, though the word itself is not prominent. He is to be notably a man of peace: not only reluctant to start strife (3:29) or to spread it (25:8,9), but disarmingly kind (see the rising sequence in 24:17,19; 25:21,22), and generous in his judgments. He will realize that silence is often wiser than criticism (11:12); that a person who has failed should evoke help rather than contempt (14:21); and that the distaste with which one views another man may owe more to one's own evil heart than to his (21:10). For all this, his kindness must not overbalance into sentimentality: he must be able to keep his distance from some (22:24,25), and able to say 'no' to an unwise transaction (6:1–5; see notes) as promptly as he will say 'yes' to a proper claim (3:27,28). The standard he upholds (12:26) will be as much a service to his neighbour as the good things he dispenses.

b. The good friend

1. *Constancy* is his first feature. Fair-weather friends are many in Proverbs (*e.g.* 14:20; 19:4,6,7), but 'there is a friend that sticketh closer than a brother' (18:24), and 'loveth at all times' (17:17). In case the reader should think only of the friendship he hopes to receive, he is urged to *give* this kind of loyalty (27:10), especially to the old friend of the family who may easily be dropped in the search for new company, but whose staunchness would stand any test.

2. *Candour.* 'Faithful are the wounds of a friend' (27:6); for 'a man that flattereth his friend spreadeth a net for his feet' (29:5). David shirked his duty to Adonijah his son ('he had not displeased him at any time in saying, Why hast thou done so?' 1 Ki. 1:6), and it cost that son his life. But any thanks that a friend gets for this service are likely to be delayed: he must be prepared to wait till 'afterwards' (28:23).

3. *Counsel.* Two sayings in chapter 27 give the two sides to this: the cheering effect of fellowship (27:9, see note; as when Jonathan strengthened David's hand in the Lord, 1 Sa. 23:16), and the healthy clash of personalities or views (27:17). A true friendship should have both elements, the reassuring and the bracing.

4. *Tact:* respect for another's feelings; refusal to trade on his affection. The examples in Proverbs are of all-too-familiar lapses: outstaying one's welcome (or forcing one's friendship on a person), 25:17; being hearty at the wrong time, when it is unwelcome (27:14) or even cruel (25:20); and not knowing when a joke has gone far enough (26:18,19).

II. THE VULNERABILITY OF FRIENDSHIP

It happens that the strongest term for a friend, *'allûp̄*, a bosom companion, usually occurs in the Old Testament in situations of betrayal (as in 2:17) or estrangement (16:28; 17:9), as if to remind us that the closest friendship needs guarding. The strains arising from thoughtlessness (as in 1*b*(4)) are the least: the real danger is from malice: the whisperer's delight in disruption (16:28), or the delight of one who holds an advantage, in pursuing it (17:9). It emerges that the qualities of the peacemaker required in a good neighbour (see 1*a*) are by no means superseded by the ties of affection. The integrity of a friendship depends as much on spiritual resources as does that of an individual.

WORDS

As many as three out of the seven abominations listed in 6:16–19 are examples of the misuse of words: such is their importance in Proverbs. What is taught about them may be grouped under three headings.

I. THE POWER OF WORDS

'Death and life are in the power of the tongue' (18:21). This power springs largely from two qualities.

1. *Penetration.* What is done *to* you is of little account beside what is done *in* you, and the latter may be for good or ill. The *feelings*, or morale, may be lacerated by a cruel or clumsy thrust ('like the piercings of a sword', 12:18a), and 'a wounded spirit who can bear?' (18:14); equally, they may be vitalized by a timely word (12:18b,25), and the whole body with them ('sweetness to the soul and health to the body', 16:24, RSV; *cf.* 15:30). One's *attitude* to another person may be deeply affected by a mere whisper, unforgettable as soon as relished (18:8), and one's *self-esteem* ruinously inflated by flattery (which entangles its victim, 29:5, by the craving it induces and by the ill-judged actions it invites). Above all, *beliefs and convictions* are formed by words, and these either destroy a man or are the making of him (11:9; 10:21).

2. *Spread.* Since words implant ideas in other minds, their effects ramify – again, for good or evil. A scoundrel's 'speech is like a scorching fire. A perverse man spreads strife' (16:27b, 28a, RSV). As in 6:14, where he 'letteth loose discord' (RVmg), his action is like Samson's incendiarism, and all may be done by 'silent, underhand procedures . . . , hints, suggestions, provocations and signals' (C. H. Toy on 6:12–14), *e.g.* by the well-timed wink or pursing of the lips seen in 10:10; 16:30. So, too, a good man will find his words bearing fruit both in the good that finds its way back to him (12:14), and in the benefits which reach out to many others, as from 'a fountain of life' (10:11; *cf.* 18:4) and 'a tree of life' (15:4). The last two metaphors lift the matter right out of the temporal sphere into the eternal (*cf.* Ps. 36:8,9; Gn. 3:22–24).

II. THE WEAKNESS OF WORDS

1. *They are no substitute for deeds.* The contrast drawn between 'toil' and 'mere talk', in 14:23, RSV (a saying to be framed and hung in council rooms), effectively balances section I.

2. *They cannot alter facts.* The most impenetrable charm has, in the end, no chance against the facts which it disguises (26:23–28); and, to look to the end, the most brazen denials (28:24) and strongest excuses (24:12) will make no impression on the final Judge.

3. *They cannot compel response.* 'By mere words a servant is not disciplined, for *though he understands*, he will not give heed' (29:19); hence the appeals to the listener to make his own search for wisdom (*e.g.* 2:3,4) as for something which the teacher cannot impart to the apathetic. ('A rebuke goes deeper into a man of understanding than a hundred blows into a fool', 17:10.) The other side of the matter is that *evil* words are subject to the same handicap. The most spicy gossip has power over the listener only in so far as he is himself 'an evildoer' and a walking 'falsehood', in whom the taste for carrion can overpower the love of truth. 'An evil-doer giveth heed to wicked lips; and a liar (Heb. *falsehood*, RVmg) giveth ear to a mischievous tongue' (17:4).

III. WORDS AT THEIR BEST

Proverbs gives teaching on (a) the marks, and (b) the making of such words.

a. The marks of them

1. They will be *honest*. 'Righteous lips are the delight of kings' (16:13) – one of the good things which the great can neither buy nor afford to be without. *Cf.* 24:24–26, where a 'right' answer (26) is literally a 'straight' or 'straightforward' one. *Cf.* also 25:12; 27:5,6; 28:23.

2. They will be *few*. This point is made with irony in 17:28 ('Even a fool may pass for wise, if he says nothing', Moffatt); but there are solid enough grounds for it elsewhere. In one's own interest, the less said, the less ammunition there is for ill-wishers (10:14; 13:3); for one's neighbour's good, reticence may save a friendship (11:12,13); and in relation to God, when words run away with a man they run him into folly and arrogance: 'When words are many, transgression is not lacking' (10:19).

3. They will be *calm*. A link with the previous paragraph is found in 17:27, where a sparing use of words is commended as the mark of 'a cool spirit', which denotes 'a man of understanding'. Three reasons can be found for this praise of calmness: first, it allows time for a fair hearing (18:13; *cf.* verse 17); second, it allows tempers to cool (15:1: 'A soft answer . . .'); and third, its influence is potent: 'a soft tongue breaketh the bone' (25:15).

4. They will be *apt*. A truth that makes no impression as a generalization may be indelibly fixed in the mind when it is matched to its occasion and shaped to its task. There is a craftsman's as well as a recipient's delight glimpsed in 15:23: 'To make an apt answer is a joy to a man, and a word in season, how good it is!' The same aesthetic pleasure glows in the language of 10:20 ('the tongue of the righteous is as choice silver') and 25:11 ('like apples of gold in a setting of silver'); *cf.* also 25·12; 22:11; 10:32.

b. The making of them

1. *Study.* 15:28 states what the foregoing paragraph implies. 'The mind of the righteous ponders how to answer, but the mouth of the wicked pours out evil things.' A similar point is made in 15:2. When we add to this the implications of 2:6 and, perhaps, 16:1, we are within sight of the classic statement in Isaiah 50:4 ('The Lord God hath given me the tongue of them that are taught . . .').

2. *Character.* Some of the apparent platitudes of the book (*e.g.* 14:5; 12:17) arise from its insistence that what a man *says* wells up from what he *is* – it will be worth what he is worth. So '*the tongue* of the righteous' is weighed against '*the heart* of the wicked', and their values ('choice silver'; 'little worth') are compared directly (10:20). It is put most forcibly in the familiar saying of 4:23: 'Keep your heart with all vigilance; for from it flow the springs of life.' It is only a step from here to our Lord's, 'Out of the abundance of the heart the mouth speaketh' (Mt. 12:34).

THE FAMILY

I. HUSBAND AND WIFE

While kings allowed themselves the doubtful luxury of polygamy the ordinary Israelite seldom resorted to it, and in Proverbs the union of one man with one woman is clearly shown to be the norm, both by the absence of any allusion to the discords of polygamy (though we meet other domestic troubles, from unfaithfulness to nagging) and by the fully personal bond taken to exist between husband and wife. The two share the children's training and are assumed to speak with one voice (1:8,9; 6:20, *etc.*); towards his partner the man is urged to be not merely loyal but ardent, 'ravished always with her love' (5:19); and a broken marriage vow is a sin against an old comrade (2:17) – the word here is *'allûp̄*, always a term for the closest of friends (*cf.* 16:28; 17:9; Ps. 55:13). This is a far cry from the not uncommon ancient idea of a wife as chattel and childbearer but no companion. Far from being a cypher, the woman is the making or the undoing of her husband (a God-given 'boon', 18:22; 19:14; indeed his 'crown'; or else 'rottenness in his bones', 12:4). On her constructive womanly wisdom chiefly depends the family's stability (14:1), and if she happens to possess exceptional gifts she will have ample scope for them: the capable wife in 31:10ff. is administrator, trader, craftswoman, philanthropist and guide, whose influence spreads far beyond her home, though it is centred there and though her achievements are (as she would wish) valued most of all for their contribution to her husband's fortune and good standing (31:11,23).

Against so high a view of marriage, sexual sin is presented in the darkest colours. It is a squandering of powers that were designed for the founding of a true family that should be one's own, and close-knit, and divinely blessed (5:9–23). It is an exchange of true intimacy for its parody (5:19,20), a parting with one's honour (5:9; 6:33) and liberty (23:27,28). It is to throw away one's best years (5:9,11) and possibly one's last possessions (29:3; 6:26, see note). It is to court physical danger and social disgrace (6:26, 32–35); and this is not all. Those who think to explore life this way are flirting with death. It is no mere detour from the best path but, in the fullest sense, a dead-end: 'for her house sinks down to death, and her paths to the shades; none who go to her come back nor do they regain the paths of life' (2:18, 19, RSV). To change the figure, it is a sin which sears the sinner inescapably: 'Can a man take fire in his bosom, and his clothes not be burned? Or can one walk upon hot coals, and his feet not be scorched?' (see 6:27–29, 33b).

II. PARENTS AND CHILDREN

Proverbs is well known for its praise of the rod. Its maxim, 'he that spareth his rod hateth his son' (13:24) is a corollary of its serious doctrine of wisdom; for if wisdom is life itself (8:35,36), a hard way to it is better than a soft way to death ('Thou shalt beat him with the rod, and shalt deliver his soul from Sheol', 23:14; *cf.* 19:18). The way has to be hard, for two reasons. First, 'foolishness is bound up in the heart of a child'; it will take more than words to dislodge it (22:15). Secondly, character (in which wisdom embodies itself) is a plant that grows more sturdily for some cutting back (*cf.* 15:32,33; 5:11,12; Heb. 12:11) – and this from early days (13:24b: 'betimes'; *cf.* 22:6: 'Train up a child in the way he should go, and even when he is old he will not depart from it'). In 'a child left to himself' the only predictable product is shame (29:15).

But the rod is no panacea. The book tacitly condemns the martinet by its own reasonable approach, its affectionate earnestness, and its assumption that the old find their natural crown, and the young their proper pride, in each other (17:6). The parents' chief resource is constructive, namely their 'law', taught with loving persistence. This 'law' (*tôrâ*) is a wide term which includes commands (*cf.* 3:1; 7:2) but is not confined to them: basically it means direction, and its aim here is to foster wise habits of thought and action (in the 'heart' and in the 'fingers', 7:3) which, so far from enslaving a person, will equip him to find his way through life with sureness (3:23; 4:12) and honour (1:9; 4:8,9). There is a childhood reminiscence of its tenderness preserved in 4:3ff., and a sample of its bracing out-spokenness, its home truths, in 31:1–9.

Many are the reminders, however, that even the best training cannot instil wisdom, but only encourage the choice to seek it (*e.g.* 2:1ff.). A son may be too opinionated to learn (13:1; *cf.* 17:21). A good home may produce an idler (10:5) or a profligate (29:3): he may be rebel enough to despise (15:20), mock (30:17) or curse (30:11; 20:20) his parents; heartless enough to run through their money (28:24), and even to turn a widowed mother out of doors (19:26). While there are parents who have only themselves to thank for their shame (29:15), it is ultimately the man himself who must bear his own blame, for it is *his* attitude to wisdom (29:3a; 2:2ff.), *his* consent given or withheld (1:10) in face of temptation which sets his course. Corresponding to the family shame is the joy which a wise son bestows; this theme opens the central portion of the book, and recurs regularly enough for Delitzsch to see in it the motif that announces each major paragraph of that collection (*e.g.* 10:1; 13:1; 15:20).

III. BROTHERS

Brothers are the subject of only a few proverbs; and it must be remembered that the Hebrew term can be used of cousins and various relatives. These are not always seen living up to their name: a poor relation, for example, found himself as unpopular in the ancient world as in the modern: 'All the brethren of the poor do hate him: How much more do his friends go far from him! He pursueth them with words, but they are gone' (19:7). When discord is sown (6:19) or an injury done in a family, the resultant feud may well have a bitterness and obstinacy all its own (18:19; see note).

But these are the diseases of brotherhood. In its healthy state it is synonymous with constancy: a brother comes into his own in bad times (17:17), and if bonds of friendship sometimes surpass those of kindred (18:24; 27:10, see note), then that is their highest praise.

IV. THE FAMILY IN GENERAL

In all, the family holds in Proverbs the pivotal place in society which it received in the Sinai Covenant when it was written into the Decalogue three times over. The family loyalties which are briefly enjoined in the latter come to life here in the homely glimpses of children faithfully brought up, and parents joyfully united; while the exposure of the suicidal nature of those sins which specially flout this divine order (1:18; 2:18) gives point to the teaching in the fifth commandment that stability ('thy days . . . long in the land'; *cf.* Pr. 4:10) is the proper product of sound family life.

LIFE AND DEATH

Among the many promises of life and warnings of death in Proverbs some are to be taken in the narrowest sense, as teaching that sound conduct and the blessing that goes with it tend to prolong a man's days, and that evil tends to shorten them. 'Receive my sayings; and the years of thy life shall be many' (4:10; *cf.* 3:2; 9:11). But often the terms that accompany them show that 'life' and 'death' are to be understood qualitatively, and at various levels. For convenience we shall look at the two words separately.

I. LIFE

a. Material and social

In 16:15 'life' denotes the flourishing of one's affairs when authority smiles, and in 15:27 to 'live' seems to mean to enjoy harmonious family life, for its opposite is not 'he shall die' but 'he . . . troubleth his own house'.

b. Personal or psychological

Wisdom and discretion are seen in 3:22 as 'life to thy soul, and grace to thy neck' – and the second of these phrases, pointing to a person's outward bearing, suggests that the first refers to the *vitality* of his whole being ('soul' in the Old Testament denotes the whole man). Certainly it means this in 14:30, where 'a sound heart' (or 'a tranquil mind', RSV) 'is the life of the flesh: But envy is rottenness of the bones'.

c. Moral and spiritual

In several places it is not too much to say that 'life' means fellowship with God. There is a revealing antithesis in 10:16, where the statement 'the labour of the righteous tendeth to life' is matched by: 'the increase of the wicked tendeth' (not, 'to death', but) 'to sin'. On the positive side, some of the major Old Testament expressions for godliness are interchangeable with 'life' or to 'live'. *Wisdom* itself is its synonym in 8:35: 'he who finds me finds life'; which is amplified in the next phrase, 'and *favour* (*rāṣôn*, acceptance; *cf.* Ex. 28:38; Is. 56:7, *etc.*) from the Lord'. In 9:6, 'forsake the foolish and live' is capped by: 'and walk in the way of *understanding*'; and in 21:21 the favourite prophetic terms *righteousness* and *steadfast love* (*ḥeseḏ*) are its equivalents. Probably also in 19:23, where the parallel to 'life' is the phrase 'shall abide satisfied', we are to understand it in a spiritual rather than a physical sense, as in the affirmation of Psalm 17:15: 'I shall be satisfied . . . with thy likeness'.

This understanding of 'life' as implying more than mere existence is expressed most tellingly in the phrases 'tree of life', 'fountain of life' and 'path' or 'way of life'.

Tree and *fountain of life* are, at the simplest level, graceful figures of God's sources of renewal, temporal and spiritual: *e.g.* of the effects of a heartening word from somebody (15:4); or of a wish that at last comes true (13:12); going deeper, they depict the wholesome influence of a good man on other people; a man who guards his 'first springs of thought and will' (to borrow Thomas Ken's allusion to 4:23) and so wins people to righteousness by his character (11:30, see note) and words (10:11). To go deeper still, this tree or fountain symbolizes the blessings of a right relation to God, variously described as wisdom (3:18), understanding (16:22) and 'the fear of the Lord' (14:27), inculcated by the 'law of the wise' (13:14). The metaphors tell their own story, but this is reinforced by the overtones of Genesis 2 and 3, where the tree bore the fruit of immortality, and the river watered the garden of God. Tree and river reappear in the end-time vision of Ezekiel 47:1–12 when the glory has returned (*cf.* Rev. 22:1,2); but the Old Testament affirms that what was lost with Paradise and waits to be regained can be enjoyed in some measure here and now when man walks with God. 'For *with thee* is the fountain of life' (Ps. 36:9; *cf.* Ps. 46:4,5).

The phrase, the *path* or *way of life*, similarly, uses the term 'life' qualitatively, either in contrast to the way that leads downward to death (*e.g.* 15:24, RSV: 'The wise man's path leads upward to life') or in parallel with terms for wisdom ('For the commandment is a lamp; and the law is light; and reproofs of instruction are the way of life', 6:23; *cf.* 9:6). The expression, 'way of life', in fact, is used not as we use it, in the sense of a mode of existence (with the emphasis on 'way'), but (with the emphasis on 'life') of a route that leads to, or is marked by, one's being truly and fully alive.

This raises the question whether or not 'life' is ever viewed in Proverbs as a goal beyond the grave. The phrase 'way of' can mean in Hebrew either 'way to' or 'way belonging to', and both these senses are present in the idea of a path which begins in the realm of true life and leads you further in (*cf.* 4:18, Moffatt: 'on and on to the full light of day'). In Psalm 16:11 'the path of life' is very probably to be seen extending into eternity, for the context shows the defeat of death; but in Proverbs there is no comparable context. The Christian knows how far the road leads, but this map does not show it. In 12:28 there is a glimpse of it – it would seem – but the unusual Hebrew construction makes translation a little tentative (see commentary). Two other verses (11:7; 14:32) point more firmly in its direction; but they do no more. (They are discussed at the end of the next section.)

II. DEATH

Proverbs uses the words 'death' and 'die' between 20 and 30 times, and refers in a further dozen places to Sheol (1:12; 5:5; 7:27; 9:18; 15:11,24; 23:14; 27:20; 30:16), Abaddon (destruction) (15:11; 27:20), the pit (1:12; 28:17) and the Rephaim (the shades) (2:18; 9:18; 21:16). Yet among all these references there are curiously few which limit their meaning beyond question to literal death. The Old Testament looks at the subject in depth: death is a whole realm in conflict with life, rather than a single and merely physical event. If we think of physical death as the centre of this realm, there is a far side, wrapped in mystery (yet open to God, 15:11), expressed in the terms Sheol, Abaddon, *etc.*, and pictured as the deep abode of the dead; but there is also a near side. Death throws its shadow over the living, in the forms of sickness (*e.g.* Ps. 116:3), calamity (Dt. 30:15) and above all, sin (Gn. 2:17); in the words of A. R. Johnson,[1] 'ideally at least, "life" is life in its fullness, and conversely any weakness in life is a form of "death".' So in Proverbs 5:23 the fate of the wicked, 'he shall die', is amplified, and evidently brought to its climax, in the next line: 'he shall go astray'; in other words, both these phrases are saying that such a man is missing *true* life; that is the real menace of death. The same point is made in the charge to a father to deliver his son from Sheol by timely discipline (23:13,14), and in the warning by wisdom, in 8:36: 'All they that hate me love death.' A man can stray into its territory and find himself among its citizens before ever he quits this earth: the sinner, in the house of folly, 'knoweth not that the dead are there; that her guests are in the depths of Sheol' (9:18).

Life after death lies beyond the horizon of Proverbs (see section I, 'Life', last paragraph, above). But there are two sayings about natural death which draw attention to some form of hope or confidence which the wicked man forfeits at that point (11:7, 'when a wicked man dieth, his expectation shall perish') and the good man retains (14:32, see commentary, 'but the righteous hath hope in his death'). Later revelation was to fill in that outline; meanwhile the bare assurance that one's labour was, in some unspecified way, 'not in vain in the Lord' inspired a hope that eventually was to seek and receive a fuller answer.

---

[1] *Studies in Old Testament Prophecy*, edited by H. H. Rowley (1950), p. 98.

ANALYSIS

COMMENTARY

TITLE, INTRODUCTION AND MOTTO (1: 1–7)

1: 1. The title

The proverbs: the opening noun (*mišlê*) gives the book its name in
the Hebrew Bible as in ours. The Heb. term (in the singular,
māšāl) basically means 'a comparison' (*e.g.* the sharp simile such
as – at random – 11:22; 12:4; or the full-grown allegory of
Ezk. 17:2 ff.; *cf.* Jdg. 9:8 ff.), but it came to stand for any kind of
sage pronouncement, from a maxim or observation (see the
middle chapters, *passim*) to a sermon (*e.g.* chapter 5), and from
a wisecrack (Ezk. 18:2) to a doctrinal revelation (Ps. 49:4). See
also the companion terms in verse 6.

Solomon: see Introduction, p. 22.

1: 2–6. The introduction: the benefits of the book

The prize it offers is wisdom (2a) and still further wisdom (5);
the path of this progress is marked by the verbs of this paragraph, which repay study; and the many aspects of wisdom are
displayed by the nouns of verses 2–5 (on which there is detailed
comment in the subject-study: Wisdom, pp. 36f.).

6. *A proverb*: see on verse 1; 'and a satire':[1] this meaning is
indicated by Habakkuk 2:6, the only other Old Testament
occurrence of the word, and by the parent verb 'to scorn', *e.g.*
1:22. *Dark sayings* is the word used of Samson's riddle (Jdg. 14:
12) and of the Queen of Sheba's tests (1 Ki. 10:1), indeed of
anything enigmatic, which needs interpreting: Numbers 12:8
(*cf.* 1 Cor. 13:12); Ezekiel 17:2; Habakkuk 2:6.

So the secondary purpose of Proverbs is to introduce the

---

[1] AV's term, *interpretation*, relates this word to the 'spokesman' or 'inter-
preter' of Genesis 42:23; Job 33:23, *etc.*, which is also possible. Another
suggestion (H. N. Richardson, *VT*, 1955, p. 178) derives it from the root
m-l-ṣ, 'to slip', hence 'an alluding (slipping away) saying'.

reader to a style of teaching that provokes his thought, getting under his skin by thrusts of wit, paradox, common sense and teasing symbolism, in preference to the preacher's tactic of frontal assault.

1: 7. The motto
This is also the motto of the Wisdom writings in general, and reappears, in substance, in 9:10; 15:33; Psalm 111:10; Job 28:28.

The beginning (*i.e.* the first and controlling principle, rather than a stage which one leaves behind; *cf.* Ec. 12:13) is not merely a right method of thought but a right relation: a worshipping submission (*fear*) to the God of the covenant, who has revealed Himself by name (*the Lord, i.e.* Yahweh: Ex. 3:13-15). *Knowledge*, then, in its full sense, is a relationship, dependent on revelation and inseparable from character ('wisdom and training', 7b). When we fence off (as we must) limited fields of knowledge for special study, the missing context must be remembered, or our knowing is precocious and distorted, as at the Fall, and we end by knowing less (*cf.* 3:7; Rom. 1:21,22), not more.

I. A FATHER'S PRAISE OF WISDOM (1: 8 – 9: 18)

1: 8-19. 'If sinners entice thee . . .'
The two ways of verse 7 are now seen to lie at the reader's feet: the vivid details, the fatherly earnestness, and the insistence that the final outcome should be faced (*cf.* note on 5:4), are typical of the teaching style of this group of chapters, 1-9. (On *the law of thy mother* (8), see note on 3:1, and subject-study: The Family, p. 49.)

The first way (8,9) has none of the flashy appeal of the second (10-19): it offers nothing material, only the hard-won beauty and authority (9; *cf.* Gn. 41:42) of goodness (*cf.* 3:22; 4:9; and note on 3:3). With the description of the second way, the sting is in the tail. The proposal of 11-14 owes its attractiveness to its offer (in common with all temptation) of a quick route to *ersatz* excitement and power (the youth pictures himself a person to be reckoned with, instead of patronized and kept in his place) and, above all, of acceptance as 'one of the gang'. After the defiant verse 11, verse 16 seems to carry little weight – until the trap is sprung in 18. Verse 19, clinching the lesson, brings out the *necessary* connection between gaining the world and losing one's soul – for to live for one's takings is even more corrupting than to wield power, since one has already, by definition, dethroned justice and mercy, to leave appetite as master.[1]

1: 20-33. Wisdom's impassioned appeal

This passage is the first of many in which wisdom[2] is personified; the most far-reaching of these is chapter 8. Here the open proclamation, heard above the noise of the market, significantly balances the domesticity of verse 8, to make it clear that the offer of wisdom is to the man in the street, and for the business of living, not to an élite for the pursuit of scholarship.

The forceful verbs of 20–24, and the depicting of lost opportunity in 24–33, create a climate of urgency; the verbs of rejection in 22,24,25, make the issue hinge solely on the individual's choice. If, elsewhere in the book, fool and scorner appear to be fixed types, it is their fault, not their fate: they are eating *of the fruit of their own way* (30,31).

21. *Concourse*: the Heb. suggests hubbub; there is no need to emend it (with RSV) to the somewhat similar Heb. word for *walls* which the LXX evidently read.

26. *I . . . will laugh* is not an expression of personal heartlessness, but of the absurdity of choosing folly, the complete vindication of wisdom, and the incontestable fitness of the disaster. *Cf.* Psalm 2:4.

---

[1] *Gain* (19) does not always imply violence (as RSV), but the Heb. phrase does depict at the least a 'money-grubbing' attitude: *cf.* 15:27; Ezk. 22:27, etc.

[2] *Wisdom* here and in 9:1; 24:7; Ps. 49:3, is spelt *ḥokmôṭ*, which is either a Phoenician form of the singular (see Introduction, p. 17; *WIANE*, p. 8) or a Heb. plural. If it is the latter, it is to express intensity and fullness; and like the plural Elohim (God), it uses a singular verb (*cf.* 9:1).

28. *Seek . . . early* (AV), or *diligently* (RV, RSV): the expression translates the single word *šiḥar*, to seek. The note of earnestness or earliness is suggested by its probable connection with *šaḥar*, dawn (*cf.* the thought, but not the terminology, of Je. 44:4; Ps. 130:6). This is supported by Proverbs 13:24b, where the thought of being in time or in earnest makes better sense than that of bare seeking.

32. *Turning away* (AV, RSV) is more accurate than RV's *backsliding*, as also in Hosea 14:4, *etc. Complacence* (RSV) is preferable to the objective *prosperity* (AV, RV). Contrast with this the justified peace of mind of the responsive, in 33.

2: 1–22. Wisdom as treasure and safeguard
2: 1–5. Wisdom, hard-won.
This is the essential counterpart to 1:20 ff., where wisdom was clamouring to be heard. Here it is the pupil who must clamour (3). Yet the search, strenuous as it must be, is not unguided. Its starting-point is revelation – specific (*words*) and practical (*commandments*); its method is not one of free speculation, but of treasuring and exploring received teachings so as to penetrate to their principles (see the verbs of 1–5); and its goal, far from being academic, is spiritual: *the fear of the Lord. . . . the knowledge of God* (5). With these two phrases verse 5 encompasses the two classic Old Testament terms for true religion – the poles of awe and intimacy.

2: 6–9. Wisdom, God-given.
What you *find*, then (5), is what He *gives* (6); discovery and revelation are inseparable. This paragraph goes on to show that to know the Lord is also to know how to live; the synonyms for wisdom lead up to *tûšiyyâ* (7), 'sound sense' or effectiveness (it can denote both the quality itself and its outcome, *cf.* subject-study: Wisdom, 1(3), p. 37). As this practical note is prominent in Proverbs, it is important to mark how verses 7–9 pile up moral nouns, to put it beyond doubt that the success in view is right conduct. These lovers of wisdom are *saints* (8: *ḥᵃsîḏîm*: loyal sons of the covenant).

2: 10–22. Wisdom, moral safeguard.
Verses 10, 11 show

how God imparts the protection envisaged in 7b, 8, and verses 12-15, 16-19, illustrate the temptations, through evil men and evil women, against which it avails.

The process is that wisdom and knowledge, when they become your own way of thinking, and your acquired taste (10), will make the talk and interests of evil men alien to you (12-15). Even *the adventuress with her smooth words* (16, RSV, see note below) will show up at once as false – as both quitter (17) and, precisely, *femme fatale* (18,19): who offers a taste of life, and sells you death.

14, 15. Various synonyms for what is 'twisted' occur throughout the book (often translated *froward(ness)* in AV). Probably both of the main implications of the idea are to be understood: *i.e.* devious(ness) and *perverse(ness)* (RV, RSV).

16. *Loose woman . . ., adventuress* (RSV). Both these terms mean lit. 'foreigner' or *stranger*; *i.e.*, in such a context (*cf.* 17b), 'one who is outside the circle of [a man's] proper relations, that is, a harlot or an adulteress' (Toy). *Cf. The Instruction of Ani* (see Introduction, p. 19): 'Be on thy guard against a woman from abroad . . . : a deep water, whose windings one knows not, a woman who is far away from her husband' (*ANET*, p. 420a).

17. *The friend* (RV; rather than AV's *guide*): *i.e.* her husband. The word denotes close companionship: *cf.* 16:28; 17:9; Psalm 55:13; *cf.* also, in a context of spiritual adultery, Jeremiah 3:4. *The covenant of her God*: *i.e.* His covenant with Israel, including in its obligations the seventh commandment. The wording of the phrase is against its referring merely to a marriage covenant as in Malachi 2:14.

18. *Sinks down* (RSV): this is the literal sense of the verb, and a vivid touch. But a grammatical difficulty suggests that we should translate it: 'she sinks down to death [which is] her home' (*cf.* RVmg). On *death*, see subject-study: Life and Death p. 55.

21, 22. *The land . . . the land* (RV, RSV): *cf.* Psalm 37:9, *etc.*, where the primary thought is of the land promised to God's people. We may translate it *earth* (AV), but viewed as the Lord's and His people's.

3: 1-35. The whole-hearted disciple

Whereas chapter 2 emphasized the moral stability which grows with wisdom, chapter 3 particularly promises serenity. This is seen as the fruit of a thoroughgoing godliness, three aspects of which mark the main divisions of the chapter.

3:1-10. Glad commitment. The kernel of this section (and of the chapter) is found in 5,6; but the childlike trust to be seen there is rooted in sound teaching (1-4) and expressed by bold obedience (*e.g.* 9).

1. *Tôrâ*, the word for *law* (AV, RV), fundamentally means 'direction'; *cf.* RSV: *teaching*. Where it occurs unqualified (28:9; 29:18) it is clearly the divine law (it is also the Jewish term for the Pentateuch); but *my law*, 'thy mother's law' (1:8), *etc.*, refer to the present maxims and to the home teachings, based indeed on the law, but not identical with it.

3. *Bind them . . . write them*: *cf.* 1:9; 6:21; 7:3 – striking expressions for glorying in, meditating on and (7:3) acting by these principles. The literalism with which later Judaism understood the similar language of Deuteronomy 6:8,9 is excluded by these verses, and indeed by Exodus 13:9.

4. *Understanding* (*śekel*, shrewdness) seems a slightly inappropriate reward here, and RSV 'corrects' it to *repute* (by reading Heb. *śēm* for *śekel*). But there seems no reason why the Heb. noun, like its parent verb, should not mean *success* (AVmg; *cf.* Ps. 111:10, AVmg) when the context suggests it. See note on 2:7, and subject-study: Wisdom, 1 (3), pp. 36f.

5. *Trust . . . lean*: these two words may be even closer together in thought than appears at first sight. G. R. Driver argues[1] that the Heb. for *trust* had originally the idea of lying helplessly face downwards – an idea preserved in Jeremiah 12:5b (see RSV) and Psalm 22:9b (Heb., 10). *Lean* is not 'incline', but 'support yourself', *rely* (RSV).

6. *Acknowledge* is quite simply 'know', which contains not only the idea of acknowledging, but the much richer content of being

[1] 'Difficult Words in the Hebrew Prophets', in *Studies in Old Testament Prophecy*, edited by H. H. Rowley (1950), p. 59.

'aware of', and having 'fellowship with'. And the promise that closes the verse offers more than guidance, though it includes it: *He will make straight your paths* (RSV), as He did for the unwitting Cyrus (Is. 45:13; *cf.* Is. 40:3) to bring him to his appointed goal.

7 ff. The cost and reward of 'knowing' God in all one's ways (6) are now illustrated, first in the personal realm (7,8: the mind and will capitulating, and the whole man invigorated) and then in the material sphere (9,10: a dedicated income becoming a multiplied one).

9. We tend to seize on verse 10, either critically or hopefully. But it must not steal the thunder of verse 9. To 'know' God in our financial 'ways' is to see that these *honour* Him; the honour will be compounded largely of homage (in giving Him the first and not a later share, 9; *cf.* 1 Cor. 16:2; Mk. 12:44), of gratitude (see Dt. 26:9–11) and of trust (*cf.* verse 5), for such giving in the face of material pressures is a simple test of faith. But a basic ingredient is fair business dealings; and this is saved up for fuller treatment in the final paragraph (27–35).

10. The generalization that piety brings *plenty* chimes in with much of Scripture (*e.g.* Dt. 28:1–14; Mal. 3:10) and of experience. If it were *more* than a generalization (as Job's comforters held), God would be not so much honoured, as invested in, by our gifts. Verses 11,12 are therefore well placed to balance 8 and 10 (and to lead into 13ff.) with the reminder of other divine methods and better prizes than prosperity.

3:11–20. Patient quest. The childlike trust of 1–10 is to coexist with the mature wisdom now held up before us. In this preview of the great chapter 8, wisdom is seen as a possession (often hard-won, 11,12) which brings all else in its train (13–18) – indeed, without which the very universe would not have existed (19,20) – and which crowns its possessor with peace (21–26).

11. *Despise*: rather, 'reject' (*cf.* 1 Sa. 15:23), which is truer to life: the natural reaction to hardship is resentment, not contempt. And *be weary* means rather 'shrink from'. This double antagonism, of will and emotions, in the two halves of the verse, is the negation of the chapter's keynote, 'trust'(5), and would make the discipline useless. *Cf.* Hebrews 12:5-11, which quotes and expounds this.

14. The word for *merchandise* (AV, RV) means both trade and the wealth it brings; so Moffatt: 'her profits'. That is, wisdom makes you a richer man than money ever will.

15. *Rubies*: probably (to be pedantic) 'corals'; certainly something reddish (La. 4:7) and proverbially precious. For us, therefore, *rubies* remains the nearest equivalent.

16. There could hardly be a neater assessment of earthly blessings, in Old Testament terms, than this. As the gifts of the *left hand, riches, etc.*, are valued highly, but not unconditionally, nor supremely; long life, from the *right hand*, is more than wealth; and wisdom, as conferring them, is more than either. The heedless may live long and in high regard (Ps. 49:16-20), but theirs are stolen blessings, without value. See, further, verse 18.

18. *A tree of life*: on this graceful metaphor, see subject-study: Life and Death, p. 54.

19, 20. This crowning truth is enlarged upon in 8:22ff. Wisdom is one and indivisible – for God and man, and for the most majestic operations (19,20) as for the most ordinary (21, 27-35).

3:21-35. Quiet integrity. It becomes very clear that wisdom means walking with God (23,26); and the paradox of this familiar metaphor is brought out by the way in which the shrewdness commended in verse 21 (*tûšiyyâ, meˊzimmâ; cf.* subject-study: Wisdom, 1 (3), (4), p. 37) rubs shoulders with the cosmic wisdom of 19,20. The promised serenity of such a life as meets us here comes, at one level, from sheer good management on God's sound principles (22,23 are the consequence of 21), and at a deeper level, from the Lord's personal care (26). The vocabulary of verse 25 is pointedly like that of 1:27, to underline the contrast between the two ways.

The genuineness of the trust (1-12) and wisdom (13-26)

already expounded will be proved by love. So the chapter closes with samples of what it means to know God 'in all thy ways' (*cf.* 6).

27, 28. The Heb. of 27a ('. . . from its owners') brings out the injustice, not merely inconsiderateness, of delay. The wording of Leviticus 19:13 stresses the former, and Deuteronomy 24:14,15 the latter. (The positive aspect of the maxim is *bis dat qui cito dat*: 'he gives twice who gives promptly'.)

29, 30. See subject-study: The Friend, p. 44.

32. *Perverse* (RV, RSV), or *froward* (AV): see on 2:14,15. The overriding reason against hankering after the ways of the unscrupulous is that one must choose between (at the two extremes) God's detestation and His 'intimate friendship' (*secret*, AV, RV; Heb. *sōḏ*: *cf.* note on 11:13). RSV puts it well: *but the upright are in his confidence.*

34. James 4:6 and 1 Peter 5:5 closely follow the LXX form of this.

35. The second line reads literally 'but disgrace is (or, will be) exalting (or, removing) fools'. 'Removing' makes sense; but various reconstructions have been suggested, to obtain a closer symmetry with the first line. The LXX ('the ungodly exalt dishonour') is textually the nearest alternative, but it is not a self-evident improvement.

On these contrasted destinies, in general terms of honour and disgrace, *cf.* Daniel 12:2,3.

4:1–27. The lifelong pilgrimage

4:1–9. Seek. This linking of three generations (verses 1, 3ff.) demonstrates how a love of the best things will be transmitted mainly by personal influence, along the channels of affection. The approach is positive: the teacher is far less interested in 'don'ts' (though they have their place: see 3:27–31) than in getting his pupil to see that he is offered the secret of being really alive (4b), and therefore to co-operate by cultivating his own love (6) of the wisdom which is that secret.

2. *Law* (AV, RV), or, *teaching* (RSV): the word 'taught', in verses 4, 11, is the parent verb, in Heb., of this noun. See on 3:1.

7. The first line, literally, means either '(The) beginning (is) wisdom; get wisdom', or, '(The) beginning of wisdom (is): Get wisdom.' The latter, which is grammatically the more probable, could be a blunt way of saying: 'What it takes is not brains or opportunity, but decision. Do you want it? Come and get it.' The second line, in tune with this and the Gospels (*e.g.* Lk. 14:33), runs, 'And with (or, at the cost of) all that you possess . . .'. *Cf.* Moffatt: 'at any cost'.

9. *Cf.* 1:9; 3:22.

4:10-19. Choose. Two paths are set before us. Verses 10-13 describe *the way of wisdom* (11) and verses 14-17 *the path* (or *way*) *of the wicked* (14,19). In verses 18,19 the two paths are compared.

11. *Uprightness* (RSV), or 'straightforwardness', means that the path will be right, in both senses of the word, *i.e.* morally (*cf.* 2:13) and practically (*cf.* 3:6b, and note). Godly ways give firm going and the best route. The thought is continued in the next verse.

14, 15. Notice the vigour and rapid succession of the verbs, taking up the urgent style of verse 13.

16, 17. There is more than irony in this picture of upside-down morality, where wickedness has become meat and drink and even duty. It is a warning against setting foot on a path which one might think adventurous and diverting, for it can lead as far as this. The Bible does not hide the fact that one can become as zealous for evil as for good. *Fall* (16, AV, RV) should be *stumble* (RSV): a key word here: *cf.* verses 12 and 19. Contrast the Christian concern: Romans 14:21.

18. *Dawn*, in the phrase *the light of dawn* (RSV, RVmg), certainly seems implied in 18a by the sense, though the word is a general term for brightness.

19. *Darkness*: better, *deep darkness* (RSV; *cf.* Ex. 10:22). The second line shows that the main contrast with verse 18 is between danger and constant bewilderment on the one hand, and safety and growing certainty on the other. Jeremiah 23:12 takes the imagery of verse 19 still further.

4:20–27. Concentrate. The constant repetition of such a call (introducing nearly every paragraph of this section of the book) is deliberate, for a major part of godliness lies in dogged attentiveness to familiar truths. So a kind of medical inspection follows, in which one's state of readiness in the various realms symbolized by heart, mouth, eyes and feet, comes under review.

23. Heart. This word most commonly stands for 'mind' (*e.g.* 3:3; 6:32a; 7:7b; *etc.*; *cf.* Ho. 7:11), but it can go beyond this to represent the emotions (15:15,30), the will (11:20; 14:14) and the whole inner being (3:5).

Verse 23, which strikingly anticipates our Lord's teaching, needs to be taken with its less famous companions, 20–22, if *life* is to have its full meaning. That is to say, true life (see subject-study: Life and Death, p. 54) is no superficial or static possession (*cf.* Lk. 12:15ff.) but the spiritual vitality which wells up as truth is made a man's own (20–22), and flows abroad (*the issues,* AV, RV = 'the outgoings'; RSV: *the springs*) wherever his renewed outlook makes itself felt. *Cf.* Mark 7:15–23; Luke 6:45; John 4:14; 7:38. (Our verse may well be 'the scripture' alluded to in the last of these references.)

24. Mouth. After the thoughts come the words (*cf.* Lk. 6:45c; Rom. 10:10); yet it is not enough to take care of the first and let the second take care of themselves. Superficial habits of talk react on the mind; so that, *e.g.*, cynical chatter, fashionable grumbles, flippancy, half-truths, barely meant in the first place, harden into well-established habits of thought.

25. Eyes. With this steady aim, minor decisions are governed by the ultimate goal, so that, *e.g.*, 'By-Path Meadow' is assessed as by-path, rather than as meadow.

26, 27. Feet. The succession of steps, by which vision is turned into action, demands practical planning. *Ponder* (AV) and *take heed to* (RSV) are better translations than RV's *make level*, of the first word of 26. AV connects it with the Heb. for scales (*cf.* 16:11) and the idea of weighing up one's course of action. RSV has the support of a verb 'to examine, search out', in the cognate language Accadian (G. R. Driver, *JTS*, 1935, pp. 150f.). But *make level* (RV), while it fits well enough here, yields little sense in 5:21, and none in 5:6 without RV's violent paraphrase.

5:1-23. Wisdom about marriage

The chapter first uncovers the corruption under the surface-charm of the seductress (1–6), then warns of the price of in-fidelity (7–14), and finally enlarges on the lasting delight of a faithful marriage, over against its pathetic alternative (15–23).

5:1-6. The seductress. 2. *Thy lips* are not merely contrasted with the honeyed lips of verse 3: they are to be a *protection* against them; for a person whose speech is true will not get very far with a specious talker.

4. *But her end . . . Cf.* 23:18: 'surely there is an end' (AV) – an 'afterwards' – and Proverbs does not allow us to forget it, whether for warning or encouragement, since nothing can be judged by its first stages. It is instructive to study this word, variously translated, in 5:11; 14:12, 13; 16:25; 19:20; 20:21; 23:18, 32; 24:14, 20; 25:8; 29:21. Here it utterly reverses the promise: the delicious ends as the disgusting; the soothing, as the murderous. The first simile of verse 4 helps us to recognize even marginal unchastity, by its bad aftertaste to the conscience; the second shows that there is more than disenchantment to be faced. This becomes explicit in verse 5.

5. For AV's *hell*, read *Sheol* (RV, RSV): it is virtually synonymous with death. The penal word for hell (Gehenna, often used by our Lord) does not occur in the Old Testament, though the fact of it begins to be glimpsed at times (*e.g.* Is. 66:24; Dn. 12:2). But *death* (5) and *life* (6) in the Old Testament mean more than non-existence and existence (see subject-study, pp. 53ff.). From Genesis 3 onwards they have the qualitative sense which is further expounded in the New Testament.

6. AV is most faithful to the text, which runs, literally: 'The way of life lest thou (or, she) ponder . . .'. ('Thou' and 'she' are indistinguishable in this tense, in both halves of the verse.) The general sense is that her ways are *shifty and slippery* (Moffatt), in order to keep serious thought at bay. On *ponder* (6a, AV), see note on 4:26. *She knoweth . . . not* (RV): or, 'she is restless',[1] *cf.* 7:11. *Cf.* 9:13, note.

5:7-14. The price of unchastity. 8. *Keep clear* (Moffatt): the New Testament echoes this practical, if seemingly unheroic, advice (2 Tim. 2: 22; Mt. 5:28, 29), which could mean, in terms of detailed decision, *e.g.* 'change your job', 'change your newspaper', 'break with that set of friends' . . .

9-14. The primary thought of these verses is not that loose living invites disease (though 11 may well include this), but that it dissipates irrevocably the powers a man has been given to invest. He will wake up to find that he has been exploited by his chosen circle, with whom he had no real ties (9, 10), condemned by his conscience (11-13), and on the brink of public ruin (14).

In 9b, *cruel* (AV, RV) is lit. 'a cruel one', implying possibly a blackmailer.

14. Knox gives the point well: 'No marvel, had I paid the last penalty, with the assembled people for my judges!' (*Cf.* Dt. 22:22-24; Jn. 8:5. It seems that this penalty was seldom if ever enforced: *cf.* 6:33.)

5:15-23. Fidelity, the better path. The interpretation of 15-17 hinges on verse 16, which AV (with Vulg.) takes positively (*Let thy fountains . . .*), but RV (*cf.* LXX) and most modern versions negatively, understanding it as a question (*Should thy springs . . .?*). With AV, the passage is saying that strict fidelity is not an impoverishing isolationism: from such a marriage, blessing streams out in the persons and influences of a true family (17: *only thine own*, *etc.*). Taken negatively, as by RV, *etc.*, it shows up the wastefulness of promiscuity. While both interpretations are possible, the second leaves perhaps too much to the reader's discretion, since the Heb. gives no sign that verse 16 differs from 17 in construction. To that extent, the Heb. text favours the AV.

Verses 18-20 turn more explicitly to the personal love of

[1] So D. W. Thomas, citing a cognate Arabic root, in *JTS*, 1936 pp. 59f.; *ibid.*, 1953, pp. 23f.

husband and wife. The language is frankly erotic, delighting in the imagery to be found in the Song of Solomon (*cf.* Ct. 4:5,12, 15). Such an emphasis is rather rare in Scripture, simply because nature already provides it, and therefore the complementary aspects of marriage need to be stressed. But it is highly important to see sexual delight in marriage as God-given; and history confirms that when marriage is viewed chiefly as a business arrangement, not only is God's bounty misunderstood, but human passion seeks (*cf.* verse 20) other outlets.

19. For *breasts*, RSV has *affection*, which can be read from the Heb. consonants, and not only closely parallels *love* in the next line, but is found, with the same verb, in 7:18. But the traditional reading, 'breasts', makes a rather more telling contrast with verse 20, and should probably be retained. *Be . . . ravished* (AV, RV) or *infatuated* (RSV) (19, 20) is the same word as the 'go astray' (AV, RV) or 'be lost' (RSV) of verse 23. As it can also describe the effects of strong drink (20:1; Is. 28:7) it might be rendered in verses 19 and 20 'be intoxicated'.

21–23. The arguments of common sense are undergirded by appeal to Yahweh's judgment and the inner contradictions of sin. On *pondereth* (21b) see note on 4:26. *Goings* (AV), or *paths* (RV, RSV) (21b), are lit. the (waggon-) tracks made by constant use; a better everyday term would be 'habits'. In verse 23, translate with RSV *for lack of discipline*; and on the final verb see note on verse 19.

6:1–35. Pitfalls for the unwary
6:1–5. Unlimited liability.
Here is one of the quite practical counsels of Proverbs, urged with great vigour. Its place in Scripture establishes prudence as one of the virtues of a godly man. It does not banish generosity: it is nearer to banishing gambling. That is, a man's giving should be fully voluntary: its amount (*cf.* 22:27) determined by him (for then its effectiveness can be judged, and competing claims on him assessed), and not wrung from him by events outside his control. Even to the recipient, an unconditional pledge may be an unintended

disservice by exposing him to temptation and to the subsequent grief of having brought a friend to ruin.

But this is not the last word. Job 17:3 uses this circle of ideas to declare that Job is too bad a risk for anybody but God – and to plead that God will take him up (*cf.* Ps. 119:122). So a bridge is made in the Old Testament between the idea of material insolvency and spiritual. Even so, and with Christ's total self-spending in mind, we remain in need of the lesson of this passage; for the New Testament never assures us that God will underwrite every spiritual escapade we care to embark on. Materially, too, the New Testament shows us Paul accepting Onesimus's past liabilities, but not his future ones (Phm. 18, 19).

1. *Friend* (AV) is parallel with *stranger*. It is a neutral term, coloured by its context, often meaning no more than 'anyone' (see subject-study: The Friend, p. 44).

3. *Humble thyself, and make sure* (AV): both these verbs are very vigorous. The former (lit. 'stamp, or tread, thyself') means either 'make thyself small', or more probably, *bestir thyself* (RVmg); the latter (lit. 'be boisterous, arrogant') = *importune* (RV, RSV), or almost, 'bully'.

6:6–11. Sloth. See the subject-study: The Sluggard, p. 43.

6. *The ant* is the harvester ant, common in Palestine: Agur draws attention to it in 30:25; and a fourteenth-century king of Shechem quotes a proverb on its pugnacity.[1]

11. *Robber* (RV) or *vagabond* (RSV) is better than AV's *one that travelleth*. Toy (*ICC*) aptly suggests 'highwayman'.

6:12–15. The mischief-maker. It is a most lively picture. With a hint here, and a wink or a gesture there, the trouble-maker can sow discord at will – until God's hour strikes for him.

12. *Worthless* (RV, RSV; AV: *naughty*) is lit. 'of Belial'. Belial always implies wickedness as well as worthlessness (*e.g.* 1 Sa. 2:12; 1 Ki. 21:10); sometimes sheer destructiveness (Na. 1:11, 15; Ps. 18:4); eventually it becomes explicitly a name

[1] *WIANE*, p. 7.

for the devil (2 Cor. 6:15), who is the father of all such qualities.
Froward (AV, RV): see on 2:14,15.

6:16-19. Seven abominations. With its appeal to Yahweh,
the list clinches the indictment of the mischief-maker (12-15),
for the crowning abomination, *he that soweth discord* (19),
matches the phrase in 14. It may have been independently
composed (notice the fresh roles of eyes, feet, *etc.*, compared
with 13).

16. *Six . . . seven* (*cf.* 'Three . . . four', in 30:15,18, *etc.*) is a
way of showing that the list, though specific, is not exhaustive.

17-19. The detestable things are expressed in character-
istically concrete, personal terms: the reader can almost catch
the superior look and the shifty talk, and may wonder when his
own hands were last employed to an innocent person's
detriment. If we try to classify them, the abominations com-
prise one sin of attitude (17a), one of thought (18a: *imaginations*,
AV, RV = *plans*, RSV), two of speech (lies unofficial, 17b, and
official, 19a), two of action (17c, 18b) and one of influence
(19b).

6:20-35. Adultery. For comments on the metaphors of verse
21, see note on 3:3; and on those of 22, see on 2:10, 11 and on
3:21-26. The Heb. for *talk* (22) has a flavour of meditation. In
verse 23, note how the parental rules and maxims of 20 are
regarded as expressions of the absolute, divine law.

24. *Evil woman*: instead of (lit.) 'woman of evil' (*'ēšet rā'*), the
LXX reads 'wife of another man' (*'ēšet rēa'*), which involves no
change of consonants. This is possible, but not compelling.
Flattery (AV, RV) is lit. smoothness, slipperiness; hence RSV: *the
smooth tongue.* On *stranger* (RV; RSV: *adventuress*), see note on 2:16.

25. *Lust not* (AV, RV) is here a warning against a step into
danger; but lust is also itself a sin of the same kind as the act
which would complete it (Mt. 5:28; *cf.* the tenth commandment).

Eyelids (AV, RV): *i.e.* her glances. RSV has, more vividly, *eye-
lashes.*

26. The first line reads lit. 'For because of a harlot, right to a roll of bread', which is an awkward but vivid way of sketching the rake's progress (*cf.* AV, RV). The RSV, with support from the ancient versions, reads: *For a harlot may be hired for a loaf of bread, but an adulteress stalks a man's very life.* (Another suggested emendation yields: 'For a harlot seeks . . .') Against these conjectures is not only their textual uncertainty[1] but their improbable sense; for whereas AV, RV give due weight to the potential cost of *both* kinds of entanglement, RSV warns against the second by shrugging off the first, in a manner which is hardly true to the material facts, or to the moral standpoint of the book.

Precious life (AV, RV): *cf.* as against her lack of compunction, I Samuel 26:21 (which hardly supports D. W. Thomas's translation, 'a person of weight'; *WIANE*, p. 283).

27–29. Physical analogies of spiritual cause and effect are always telling; *cf.* a notable group in Amos 3:3–8. Here the thought is of inescapable punishment (AV's *innocent*, 29, is misleading: the regular meaning is *unpunished*, as in RV, RSV). What the adulterer is embracing is *fire*. In the well-known saying of Ecclesiasticus 13:1, 'He that toucheth pitch shall be defiled', the reference is to corruption of character, rather than to punishment; it continues: 'And he that hath fellowship with a proud man shall become like unto him.'

30–35. The lesson is pressed home by a comparison. A thief, even when he is pitied (for verse 30 makes better sense as statement – AV, RV – than as question – RSV), must pay up heavily (the *sevenfold* is probably a figure of speech: *cf.* Ex. 22:1); but an adulterer has disgraced himself for ever (33) and made an implacable enemy; *cf.* 27:4; Song of Solomon 8:6b. The last phrase of verse 32 perhaps glances at the death-penalty of Deuteronomy 22:22 (*cf.* Pr. 5:14), but verses 33–35 contemplate his continued, if precarious, existence. He destroys himself spiritually (*cf.* 2:18; also I Tim. 5:6).

The picture of the adulterer as social outcast may seem

---

[1] G. R. Driver, however (*VT*, 1954, p. 244), approximates to RSV without emendation, by translating 'because of' as 'the price of'. Yet one would hardly put it that the price '(mounts) up to' so small a sum.

greatly overdrawn. If so, the adjustment that must be made is to say that in any *healthy* society such an act is social suicide. Condonation, as distinct from forgiveness, only proves the adulterer to be part of a general decadence: *cf.* Jeremiah 5:7-9; 6:15.

7:1-27. Simpleton and seductress

The argument of the chapter resembles that of 6:20-35, presented, however, not in generalizations but dramatically.

7:1-5. Prologue. It is shown once more that the best advice is useless against strong temptation unless it is thoroughly taken to heart and translated into habits. Concern for it is to be as sensitive as one's care for the pupil (*apple*) of the eye (2; *cf.* another telling use of this figure in Dt. 32:10). On verse 3, see on 3:3.

7:6-23. Drama. *a. The victim* (6-9). Young, inexperienced, featherbrained, he is the very sort to need arming with borrowed wisdom. He wanders into temptation, where place (8) and time (9) can join forces against him; and if *he* is aimless, his temptress is not.

b. The huntress (10-12). Outwardly, she keeps nothing back; she is dressed, as we say, to kill; inwardly, she gives nothing away (10b, lit. 'guarded of heart', meaning either hard, unyielding, or close, secretive). It will be an unequal contest.

c. The tactics (13-21). First, comes shock treatment (13); second, a circumstantial story – it is a special day, a celebration[1]; it would be unthinkable to refuse (14). Third, flattery: he is the very one she had to find (15); fourth, sensuous appeal (16-18; in 16, read with RSV, *coloured spreads*, for AV's *carved works*); fifth, reassurance (19, 20). The whole is pressed home with a flood of words.

[1] On the *sacrifices of peace offerings* (RV, 14), see Lv. 7:16-18. It was a festive occasion, and the feast must not wait. With the adulteress's bland secularizing of her religion we may compare the pagan's bibulous Christmas; *cf.* note on 17:1. See also 21:27.

d. The kill (22,23). AV, RV's *straightway* (22) is inaccurate and misleading. RSV rightly has *all at once*, which paints vividly the sudden yielding after indecision.

The Heb. text of 22b is very doubtful (RV preserves it; AV transposes it; ancient versions find a dog, a stag (both in LXX) and a lamb (Vulg.), in texts not unlike the existing Hebrew; Toy glimpses a calf), but the general sense of 22,23 is clear.

Verse 23a refers to the unwitting beast, and 23c to the bird of 23b; but clearly a comparable fate is in store for the adulterer. For the meaning of death in such a context, see subject-study: Life and Death, p. 55, and *cf.* 2:18; 5:5; 6:32; 9:18.

7:24–27. Epilogue. After watching the young man, we are made to see ourselves as conceivably filling the same role. The defence is threefold. First, guard your mind (*heart*, 25a; *cf.* 4:23, note); you are in danger as soon as your thoughts wander in this fatal direction. Second, keep away, literally as well as in mind (25b). Third, look past her, to the casualties and *the chambers of death* (26,27) (On *hell* (*Sheol*) and *death*, see note on 5:5.)

8:1–36. Wisdom's apologia
The praise of wisdom, which has welled up at many points already, now breaks out in full flow, in a sustained appeal of great beauty and immense range. The increasing boldness of the thought, culminating in 22–31, is not designed to preoccupy the reader with metaphysics but to stir him to decision: the true climax is the 'Now therefore . . .' passage of 32–36.

The progress of the thought may be traced somewhat as follows: wisdom is (a) the would-be guide of Everyman (1–5), (b) the partner of morality (6–13), (c) the key to all success (14–21), (d) the very principle of creation (22–31), and (e) the one necessity of life (32–36).

8:1–5. Wisdom as guide for Everyman. A chapter which is to soar beyond time and space, opens at street-level, to make it clear, first, that the wisdom of God is as relevant to the shopping-centre (2,3) as to heaven itself (22); second, that it is available to the veriest dunce (5; *cf.* 1:20–33, especially 22); third, that it is active in seeking us – so that our own search, earnest as it has to be (17,34), is a response, not an uncertain quest.

8:6–13. Wisdom as morality's other self. If verses 1–5 make wisdom quite down-to-earth, 6–13 show it to be anything but 'worldly'. By definition, wisdom and godliness wholly coincide (see the motto text, 1:7), and this passage expounds wisdom's self-evident moral excellence in terms of *right* as against wrong (see the nouns of 6–9,13), and of true value (10,11).

6. *Excellent* (RSV: *noble*) *things* are lit. 'nobles' or 'princes', which seems as harsh in Heb. as in English (*cf.* 22:20, note). Some would emend the Heb. rather drastically to 'straight things', as in 9a. Köhler (in his lexicon) reaches the same meaning by a smaller but still unsupported change.

9. *Plain* (AV, RV) is better translated *straight* (RSV); it is not a truism but an expansion of verse 8. Wisdom's moral rightness is best appreciated by those who have made some progress in her paths.

10, 11. The glowing language (on *rubies*, 11, AV, RV, see note on 3:15) speaks with sober truth. *Things* (AV, RV) can be misused – the rarer they are, the more dangerously – or stultified (*cf.* 11:22). But 'discipline' (10a), *knowledge* and *wisdom* equip the user to make good use of what he has, and so to prosper (this is developed in 14–18) and, better still, to be and do good (see note on 19).

12, 13. These two verses are necessary partners. True wisdom is canny and resourceful (on *prudence*, or shrewdness, and *discretion* – AV's *witty inventions* – see subject-study: Wisdom, 1 (4), p. 37), yet being rooted in the fear of the Lord (13; *cf.* 1:7) it is free of the faults of worldly wisdom. (*Cf.* Mt. 10:16.) Notice *hate*, twice (13), the second time spoken by wisdom. What is repugnant to godliness is repugnant to wisdom: there is no conflict of interests.

8:14-21. Wisdom's rewards. From 14 to 17a, the possessive and personal pronouns, *mine*, *I*, *me*, are emphatic, so that wisdom itself, not its beneficiaries (14–17) nor its benefits (18–21), may dominate the scene. On verse 17's assurance to the seeker, *cf.* James 1:5–8, and see note on 1:28.

Are the benefits material or immaterial? Certainly both, but predominantly the latter. If men in authority (15, 16) need wisdom, it is for justice, not advantage. If *riches* (18) are conferred by it, they are coupled with *honour* and *righteousness* (and though righteousness could have its secondary meaning, *prosperity*, in 18 – so RSV – it must have its primary, moral sense in 20, where RSV concurs). Verse 19 puts the matter beyond doubt, and goes even further than 10,11. Wisdom not only excels gold as the source takes precedence over the product; wisdom's *product* is better than gold. That product may include prosperity, but only as part of a far bigger whole, which will be specified in 35 as life and divine favour.

8:22-31. Wisdom's role in creation. The section is ushered in by the emphatic *The Lord*. Here is wisdom's prime credential, presented with wonderful artistry.

First, wisdom is what Yahweh as Creator counted primary and indispensable. Second, wisdom is both older than the universe, and fundamental to it. Not a speck of matter (26b), not a trace of order (29), came into existence but by wisdom. Third, wisdom is the spring of joy, for joy breaks out whenever (30b) and wherever (31) the Creator's wisdom is exercised. Joy of creating and joy of existence – the Maker's and the creature's delight – both flow from the exercise of divine wisdom; that is, from God's perfect workmanship.

The important and keenly-debated question arises: Is wisdom here conceived as a hypostasis (*i.e.* an actual heavenly being) or as a personification (*i.e.* an abstraction, made personal for the sake of poetic vividness)?

To the present commentator, the context points to the latter. Not only does the next chapter proceed immediately to a fresh portrait of wisdom, in a new guise (as a great lady (9:1-6) whose rival (13–18) is certainly no hypostasis), but the present passage makes excellent sense at the level of metaphor: *i.e.* as a powerful way of saying that if *we* must do nothing without wisdom, God Himself has made and done nothing without it. The wisdom by which the world is rightly used is none other than the wisdom by which it exists.

But if this is how the poem should be read in its immediate context, there is also a wider setting. The New Testament shows by its allusions to this passage (Col. 1:15–17; 2:3; Rev. 3:14) that the personifying of wisdom, far from overshooting the literal truth, was a preparation for its full statement, since the agent of creation was no mere activity of God, but the Son, His eternal Word, Wisdom and Power (see also Jn. 1:1–14; 1 Cor. 1:24,30; Heb. 1:1–4).[1]

Further details call for comment.

22. *Possessed* (Vulg., AV, RV), or *created* (LXX, Targ., RSV)? The Arians (who denied the deity of Christ) appealed to LXX's 'created', to prove that Christ, the Wisdom of God, was not eternal. But our concern must be with the word's normal meaning, and with the general sense of the passage.

Elsewhere this verb (*qānâ*) predominantly means 'get', and hence 'possess' (see, *e.g.*, Pr. 4:5, 7, where wisdom is the object, as here). Of its 84 Old Testament occurrences, only six or seven allow the sense 'create' (Gn. 14:19,22; Ex. 15:16; Dt. 32:6; Pss. 74:2; 139:13; Pr. 8:22), and even these do not require it. The derived nouns still more strongly emphasize possession.

Ugaritic literature, however, has recently swung opinion towards 'create' (in spite of *Keret* II:4), because of the phrase *qnyt 'elm*, translated by C. H. Gordon as 'creatress of the gods'. But W. A. Irwin (*JBL*, 1961, pp. 133ff.) points out that both

---

[1] Judaism also divined that there were further truths latent here, drawing out from this passage the pre-existence of the law (Ecclus. 24: 9,23) and the all-pervading activity of God's Spirit (Wisdom of Solomon 1: 6,7; 7: 22ff.), viewed as a mediator between the transcendent God and His world. Philo Judaeus (born *c.* 20 BC) also made much use of the concept of wisdom, or rather reason (Gk. *logos*, which also means 'word'), as cosmic mediator, in his attempt to interpret Hebrew thought in terms of Greek.

this expression and Eve's in Genesis 4:1 imply *parenthood*, not creation (*cf.* Dt. 32:6); and C. H. Gordon has accepted this, adding, 'I agree fully . . . that Gn. 4:1 and Pr. 8:22 refer primarily to bearing or begetting children' (*ibid.*).

To sum up: this word expresses getting and possessing, in ways that vary with the context. Goods are possessed by purchase, children by birth (*cf.* our idiom, to 'have' a baby), wisdom – for mortals – by learning. And wisdom for God? To say that at first He lacked it and had to create or learn it, is both alien to this passage and absurd. It comes forth from Him; the nearest metaphor is that of birth (*cf.* 24,25). But *possessed* is perhaps (as Irwin concludes) the most serviceable word for the translator here, leaving the succeeding verses to speak more explicitly.

In the beginning of his way (AV, RV). *Beginning* can mean what is first in importance (*cf.* 1:7) or first in sequence (*cf.* Gn. 1:1), and the two senses often coexist. The latter seems to predominate here (*cf.* 'before . . . before', 25); but there is no preposition, and the phrase could mean 'As the beginning . . .'. *Way* is gratuitously changed to *work* by RSV, perhaps under the influence of the Ugaritic *drkt*, 'power, dominion'.[1]

23-25. While verse 22 has stolen the limelight, the adjacent verbs state the matter in terms of wisdom's installation in office (23a; *cf.* Ps. 2:6) and its birth (24,25). The latter verb, indeed, by its repetition, is the predominant one; and the passage as a whole may be meant to bring to mind a *royal* birth.[2]

Depths (24) is the plural of the word *t*^e*hôm* (*cf.* 28, and Gn. 1:2), which, with *beginning* (22), is an echo of the creation narrative.

26b. *Beginning* (RV; not, as AV, *highest part*) is the same word as found in 23b. See also the summary of this part of the chapter, p. 78 above.

30. 'Craftsman' (*'āmôn*): this meaning (*cf.* RV, RSV) is supported by tradition (LXX, Syr., Vulg.), by Jeremiah 52:15 (*cf.*

---

[1] For further discussion of the phrase, see Irwin, *ibid.*; J. de Savignac, *VT*, 1954, pp. 429ff.; W. F. Albright, *WIANE*, p. 7.
[2] So H. Cazelles, in *Sacra Pagina*, edited by Coppens, I, pp. 511ff.

RSV, RVmg; but AV, RV emend), and perhaps by Song of Solomon 7:1 (Heb., 2). It also makes good sense, since without it there would be no mention of wisdom's instrumentality. 'Nursling', *cf.* AV, is also possible, and would fit into a sequence from birth (24) to happy play (30b,31). But it makes wisdom's role completely irresponsible; and if this is done to avoid unduly exalting her, it is overdone.[1]

His delight: 'his' is lacking in the Heb. text. Perhaps (as in the expression 'I am prayer', Ps. 109:4) the meaning is 'I was happiness itself'.

8:32–36. Wisdom's appeal driven home.

The appeal has behind it the force of all that is fundamental (22 ff.) and joyful (30,31); now it is clinched by the ultimate sanctions, life and death.

32. *Sons* (RV, RSV), rather than AV's *children*. *Happy* (RSV), rather than *blessed* (AV, RV).

35, 36. These verses disclose their full meaning in relation to Christ, the Wisdom of God: *cf.* 1 John 5:12.

Life . . . death: see subject-study: pp. 53ff.

Sinneth against: the verb is closely matched with *findeth* (35), and almost certainly bears its basic meaning, 'to miss' (*cf.* Jdg. 20:16), as in RSV. Lit. 'my finder . . . my misser'

9:1–18. The rival feasts

In a strikingly symmetrical chapter the first and last six verses describe the rival feasts of wisdom and folly (note the almost identical 4 and 16), while the centrepiece (7–12) gives character-sketches of typical products of these opposing camps: the scoffer, with his closed mind, and the wise man, ever teachable and ever progressing.

9:1–6. The feast of wisdom.

What wisdom constructs is spacious and enduring (1), what it offers is princely (2); the incongruous feature (and our Lord took this up) is the company,

---

[1] For further discussion linking this with 'the Amen' of Rev. 3:14, see R. B. Y. Scott, *VT*, 1960, pp. 212ff.; also J. de Savignac, *VT*, 1962, pp. 211ff.

called in from the streets, the guests' deficiency their only qualification (4).

1. *Wisdom* is *ḥokmôṯ* here; see note on 1:20.

Her seven pillars have provoked ingenious but inconclusive discussion. Among recent theorists, W. F. Albright has argued for an allusion here to heathen seven-pillared shrines (*WIANE*, p. 9), to which the house of wisdom offers the true answer (just as, according to G. Boström,[1] wisdom herself is presented as the opposite of Aphrodite). More prosaically, the pillars may represent no more than a recognizable structural feature of a large and well-built house. But there may be a cosmic allusion, to the seven days of creation or to the sun, moon and five known planets, and so to the structure of the universe (*cf.* 8:27ff.). The discovery of Sennacherib's seven-pillared house for the Assyrian new-year festival could be adduced in support of either of these latter theories, the architectural or the cosmic.[2]

5. *Come, eat . . . drink*: God's invitation has always been capable of expression in these terms (*cf.* Is. 55:1,2); only the gospel reveals the full cost and substance of it: John 6:51,55.

6. 'Forsake fools': fools (simpletons, as in 4) are the object (AV), not the subject (RV) of this transitive verb. There is no need to emend 'fools' to 'folly' (*cf.* RSV), for the feast represents more than a new outlook: it is a changed pattern of life in new company.

9:7-12. The closed or open mind. This collection of maxims does not give the impression of having been written specifically for this context; some scholars would therefore delete it or (as Moffatt) relegate it to the end. But its subject and position are both significant. Its position allows the chapter (and section of the book) to end on a shattering climax (18); its content corrects the impression that men are saved or lost merely through an isolated, impulsive decision. The choice is seen ripening into character and so into destiny.

[1] *Proverbiastudien* (1935), pp. 15ff., cited by G. von Rad, *Old Testament Theology*, I, p. 444.
[2] *OTMS*, pp. 215-6.

7, 8. *Shame* (AV, RV): better, *abuse* (RSV). The further one goes with folly or wisdom, the less or the more will one put up with the criticism which is wisdom's teaching-method. 'Whosoever hath, to him shall be given . . .' (Mt. 13:12–16).

9. *Cf.* Ptahhotep (see Introduction, p. 18): 'The (full) limits of skill cannot be attained, and there is no skilled man equipped to his (full) advantage'.[1]

Wise and *righteous* (RV, RSV) are interchangeable, and verse 10 explains why.

10. On this motto of the Wisdom Writings, see on 1:7, and note Moffatt's striking translation of line 2: 'To know the Deity is what knowledge means.'

Holy (AV) is (as in 30:3) plural and without the article; so the phrase could mean 'knowledge such as saints (or, angels, *cf.* Jb. 15:15; Ps. 89:7) possess' (*cf.* AV, LXX, Vulg.); but the parallelism (which is closer still in Ho. 11:12 (MT, 12:1)) suggests that here is a term for God (*cf.* RV, RSV, Moffatt). The plural (see note on 1:20) can express excellence or comprehensiveness, like the plural word for Deity: Elohim.

11. The *for* introduces a supporting argument for the identity of wisdom and righteousness (see on 9,10): the righteous course is in fact the prudent course (*cf.* Dt. 32:47). The New Testament adds an eternal dimension to such statements.

12. This is perhaps the strongest expression of individualism in the Bible. Such statements (*cf.* Ezk. 18; Gal. 6:4,5) are not meant to deny that people benefit or suffer from each other's characters (*cf.* 10:1), but to emphasize that the ultimate gainer or loser is the man himself. Your character is the one thing you cannot borrow, lend or escape, for it is you. *Cf.* 14:10.

9:13–18. The feast of folly. 13. *A foolish woman*: RVmg's alternative, *Folly*, can be defended (*cf.* examples in Gesenius, §130e), and makes for symmetry with verse 1; but probably we should see over against the personified wisdom of verses 1–6, a very concrete embodiment of folly, in the person of the harlot.

Simple (13b, AV, RV) is lit. 'silliness', emphasizing that for all

[1] *ANET*, p. 413b.

her wiles, she shares her victims' basic deficiency. RSV's emendation, *wanton*, can claim support, but not necessity. On the other hand, *knoweth nothing* (AV, RV) is grammatically suspect in Hebrew (yet *cf.* Ne. 2:12, Heb.); LXX's *knows no shame* (so RSV) represents a fairly small difference of Heb. text, and is perhaps the right reading. A further possibility (see on 5:6) is: '*and is ever restless*'.

14. *She sits at the door*: it has an air of slovenliness; whereas wisdom, despite her importunate appeals, is always the great lady.

17. *Stolen waters are sweet* . . . Eve had to be convinced that the sweetness would survive the stealing; we have fallen far enough to be persuaded that it depends on it. If verse 10 is the motto of the wise, here is that of the sophisticated. See further 20:17; Isaiah 5:20.

18. *The dead . . . hell* (AV): rather, with RSV and margin, *the shades . . . Sheol* (see subject-study: Life and Death, p. 55). *Cf.* 2:18; 5:5; 7:27, for the same contrast between the promise of glamour and life, and the pathetic reality.

II. PROVERBS OF SOLOMON (10:1 – 22:16)

10:1. '. . . Bound up in the lad's life'
It is the other side of the truth of 9:12. Your choice may be lonely; it cannot be private. This fact throws its own light on the problem of unmerited suffering, by its reminder that without the ties (at their best, the love) by which people are members of each other, life would be less painful but immeasurably poorer.

Cf. 15:20; 27:11; 28:7; 29:3.

10:2, 3. Righteousness is the best security
Such sayings are true at four levels – logical, providential, spiritual, eternal – though the fourth is beyond the normal horizon of Proverbs (but see 11:7; 14:32, AV, RV). That is, (a) sin, seen as folly, sets up strains in the structure of life which can only end in breakdown; (b) however much rope God gives us,

He remains in control; (c) whatever their worldly state, the righteous are the truly rich (*cf.* 20–22); (d) in the world to come, justice will be complete. See also on 13:21, and subject-study: Life and Death, pp. 53ff.

Cf. Ptahhotep (see Introduction, p. 18): 'Wrongdoing has never brought its undertaking into port. (It may be that) it is fraud that gains riches, (but) the strength of justice is that it lasts'.[1]

Soul (*nep̄eš*) (3, AV, RV) is not contrasted with the body, but means the life, the person, even the appetite (23:2), according to context. *Substance* (AV) should be *craving* (RSV), or *desire* (RV).

10:4, 5. Hard work – its material and moral aspects

The two sayings are happily paired. Together, they balance the quietism of verse 3, while 4 is reinforced by 5. You might retort to verse 4 that you are not interested in getting rich, to which verse 5 replies that if poverty is no disgrace, slackness is; and you have the good name of others to consider (*son*) besides your own.

Wise (5, AV, RV), or *prudent* (RSV) is *maśkîl* (see subject-study: Wisdom, 1(3), p. 36). *Diligent* means, basically, sharp: hence, 'keen' is near the mark.

10: 6, 7. Goodness brings lasting blessing

The translation, *violence covereth the mouth, etc.* (AV, RV) is preferable to RSV, which reverses subject and object: see discussion at verse 11. The covered mouth calls to mind possibly the leper (Lv. 13:45) or the mourner (Ezk. 24:17), though the verb in those places is 'wrap'. Haman's covered face (Est. 7:8) was a token of impending death. But it is simpler to take it as the man's evil, written, as we say, all over his face. The contrasted *blessings*, which are equally plain to see, may be thought of as invoked by grateful neighbours (*cf.* 11:26) or sent direct from God (*cf.* verse 22). Blessing and shame alike live on (7).

See also 21:24; 22:1.

[1] *ANET*, p. 412b.

10: 8. The obedient and the opinionated

Even in human fields of learning it is the second-rater who tends to 'talk big'. *Fall* (AV, RV) is too neutral: rather, 'be thrust, or trodden, down'. (The second line recurs in the Heb. text of 10, where see note.)

10: 9. Nothing to hide, nothing to fear

The brother to this verse, 28:18, shows the sudden collapse of a career based on deception. *Surely* (AV, RV): the Heb. word suggests a state of mind: 'confidently', 'carefree'. *Known* (AV, RV): Prof. D. W. Thomas holds that this word should often be translated 'humiliated', which would suit this context. But RSV's *found out* fits like a glove.

10: 10. Mischief sooner made than mended

As the verse stands (AV, RV, RSVmg) it means that a tiny gesture can do great damage, and a talkative fool become intolerable. But the second line seems to have drifted here from 8b, and the LXX may preserve the true text, with the striking antithesis: 'a frank rebuke will make for peace' (Moffatt). RSV accepts it.

10:11. Sweet water and bitter

The *fountain* (RV, RSV; not *well*, AV) *of life* is traced to its ultimate source, the Lord, in Psalm 36:9, but is seen springing up in the good and wise man here and in 13:14; 14:27; 16:22. The delightful metaphor is enlarged upon in Ezekiel 47:1–12, where miraculous waters are to stream from the sanctuary, 'and everything will live where the river goes'. Jesus used this to illustrate the gift of the Spirit: John 4:14; 7:38,39. (See also 3:11–20, note on verses 13–18 and subject-study: Life and Death, p. 54.)

Violence, etc., is an identical line with 6b. The word itself would be better translated 'malice' or 'mischief' (used of perjury in Ex. 23:1), and grammatically it may be either subject or object here. RSV has the latter (*the mouth of the wicked conceals violence*), which is certainly suggested by the *order* of the Hebrew words. But the same order occurs in the next verse, where the corresponding word to 'violence' is clearly the subject. This fact, together with the better parallelism it yields, here and in 6 (where see note), seems decisively in favour of AV, RV.

10:12. Troublemaker – peacemaker

Covers does not mean 'makes up for' (as the verse is popularly quoted to imply). Its meaning is clear from its antitheses: *stirs up* (here), 'reveals secrets' (11:13), 'harps on a matter' (see 17:9, RV). This stress on conciliation is balanced by other passages warning us against hushing up our own sins (28:13) or shirking the giving of a rebuke (*e.g.* 27:5,6). It is quoted in I Peter 4:8, and perhaps alluded to in I Corinthians 13:7 (where 'bears' can means 'covers') and James 5:20.

10:13. Man – God's mouthpiece or God's mule

The first line is not tautology: *cf.* 'out of the abundance of the heart . . .' – *i.e.* if your mind is enlightened wisdom will over-flow into your words, and so into other lives (*cf.* verse 11). If your mind is closed, God will still deal with you, but by force: *cf.* Psalm 32:8,9.

10:14. Proper reticence

Lay up means here 'keep in store for the right occasion': *i.e.* it refers to discretion, not to erudition. The second line ends literally: 'is imminent destruction': so RSV, *brings ruin near*.

10:15. Don't despise money

Balance this with 2 and 16. You may be called to forgo wealth; you must certainly rate it below honesty. But don't affect to despise it; don't embrace poverty out of laziness or romanticism. (For further harsh facts to face, see 14:20; 18:23; 19:7; 22:7.)

10:16. Earnings – their use and abuse

Note the contrast between *life* and *sin*, underlining the spiritual connotation of the former, as so often in Proverbs (see subject-study: Life and Death, p. 53). The lesson is that one is not to blame poverty or wealth for the quality of one's life. A man uses his possessions according to his character: as tools for good or ill. (*Labour*, AV, RV: rather, *wage*, RSV: in Heb. a single word often stands for a thing and its result; its parallel in the second line is, lit., 'income'.)

10:17. Stay teachable, you stay progressive

The expression *to life* (Heb., RSV) is common to this verse and its predecessor, emphasizing the fact that life is not mere existence, but a quality to attain. Note that the contrast is between keeping and forsaking: *i.e.* not only must instruction be listened to; it must be held fast over a long period.

10:18. The hater's dilemma

Have hatred in your heart, and you must play either the humbug or the fool in your words. (LXX has 'righteous' instead of *lying*; hence Moffatt, freely, 'The good man will not vent his hate.' But the Heb. text makes satisfactory sense.)

10:19-21. Words, good and bad

19. Use them sparingly!

20. They are worth what *you* are worth. (Note the parallelism between *tongue* and *heart*, AV, RV.)

21. They are what you make of them. (The righteous will get nourishment enough to feed others; the fool not enough even for himself.)

10:22. Wealth unspoilt

The Heb. adds an emphatic pronoun (as in AV, RV): '*it* makes rich' – *i.e.* nothing else does. (The marginal alternative to the second line in RV, RSV is a little forced, and yields a questionable sense. Toy points out that Psalm 127:2 'affirms not that labour in itself is useless, but only labour unattended by the divine blessing'.)

10:23. Taste – depraved or sound

The AV (=RVmg) isolates the second line too much from

the first for the syntax and the sense, and makes it nearly tautologous. Follow RSV's expansion of RV: *but wise conduct is pleasure to . . .* This line answers (and the first line accounts for) the worldly taunt of 'killjoy'.

(Some commentators take *to do mischief* (AV) as the subject of the whole sentence, and emend *wisdom* to 'abomination' or 'poison'. So Moffatt: 'but to a man of sense it is disgusting'. There is no textual support for this.)

10:24, 25. The insecurity of the wicked

The fear (24, AV, RV) is the thing dreaded (*cf.* 28), not the emotion; so RSV, *What the wicked dreads.* Within this life, it often holds good. In the ultimate sense, it is inescapable, for what the wicked man shrinks from is, in the end, God; and he must stand before Him. *The desire of the righteous* is also, ultimately, God; and 'they shall see his face'. 'In the end, that Face which is the delight or the terror of the universe must be turned upon each of us either with one expression or the other, either conferring glory inexpressible or inflicting shame that can never be cured or disguised.'[1]

25. *As . . . so* (AV): rather, 'when . . . then', *cf.* RV, RSV. This verse and 24 are brought together in 1:27. The wicked man bases everything on what is temporal; he knows that he is finished if that goes. *Cf.* Psalm 1; Matthew 7:24–27.

10:26. The exasperating sluggard

See subject-study: The Sluggard, pp. 42f.

10:27-30. Massive certainty

In general, see notes on verses 2,3.

29. It is best to take the verse as having a single subject, so that what is a *stronghold* (rather than *strength*, AV) to the righteous is 'ruin' (Moffatt; or 'dismay', 21:15, RSV) to the wicked. The Heb. consonants allow either *the way* (RV) or *the Lord* (RSV) to be subject; the latter matches *stronghold* better than the former,

---

[1] C. S. Lewis, 'The Weight of Glory', *Transposition* (1949), p. 28.

and is thereby preferable. For this two-edged effect *cf.* Hosea 14:9; John 15:22; 2 Peter 2:21.

30. *The land* (RV, RSV): see on 2:21,22.

10:31, 32. The fruit of the lips

31. Moffatt brings out the sense of the first verb by 'puts forth buds of wisdom'. *Froward(ness)* (AV, RV), here and in 32, from a root 'to turn, or twist', has *perversity* as its main idea, with a suggestion of crookedness as well.

32. Here is speech with grace as well as truth, while perversity is seen as opposed to not only what is wise (31) but what is pleasant.

11:1. Short weight

The Law (Lv. 19:35f.), the Prophets (Mi. 6:10f.) and the Wisdom Writings (see also 20:10,23) agree in condemning dishonesty primarily for *God's* sake. For the same reason we are encouraged to give not only in full but to overflowing (Lk. 6:35–38). See also 16:11, and note.

11:2. Pride pricked

This word for *pride* is from a root that suggests boiling up, and is used of the arrogance of those who must have everything their own way, and will not be 'kicked around': *e.g.* Pharaoh (Ne. 9:10), Israel (Ne. 9:16,29), the social rebel (Dt. 17:12,13), the bogus prophet (Dt. 18:20), the murderer (Ex. 21:14). *Lowly* (AV, RV) is a rare word, found only here and (as a verb) in Micah 6:8 ('walk humbly with thy God'), where it suggests the biddable spirit that is the opposite of the insubordination just considered.

11:3–9. Righteousness sees a man through

Verses 3 and 5 relate righteousness to the perplexing choices of life, and the rest of the group, to its perils. A spectacular illustration of 3a, 5a, is the career of Joseph, his integrity the best of guides; but what matters is that the honest thing to do is by definition (9:10) the wise one. On the safety which righteousness offers (4,6–9), see the comment on 10:2,3, and the subject-study: Life and Death, pp. 53ff.

6. *Treacherous* (RSV), or 'renegades', is more accurate than AV's 'transgressors', and the final phrase should probably be translated *by their lust* (RSV).

8. The meaning may be that the wicked are caught in their own trap, like Pharaoh's host or Daniel's enemies (*cf.* 28:10), but it may go further than this: see note on 21:18.

9. *Godless* (RV, RSV), or 'apostate', should replace AV's *hypocrite*. Moffatt takes his talk to be slanderous, but the second line suggests that it is, rather, subversive, undermining true values. The best defence is *knowledge*, at first hand, so that you by-pass his distortions.

11:10, 11. A people's happiness
However drab the world makes out virtue to be, it appreciates the boon of it in public life: *cf.* 14:34; 28:12. *Blessing* (11) may be either the blessing they invoke (*cf.* the second line) or the success they attract (*cf.* Gn. 30:27; 39:5).

11:12, 13. Least said, soonest mended
12. The most misleading way to feel wise is to feel superior (14:21 goes further: it is sin), for one is denying that God is the only competent judge of human worth. RSV has aptly *he who belittles*, implying, as does the second line, the further folly of voicing such a judgment.

13. Other Old Testament references to the *talebearer* (apart from the indeterminate 20:19) portray him as malicious rather than indiscreet; he is an informer, out to hurt: see *e.g.* Leviticus 19:16; Ezekiel 22:9. This gives added point to the first line: *i.e.* he will deliberately betray you. *Secrets* (*sôḏ*) is a word with some-times the sense of 'council' (so LXX here), sometimes the informal sense of an intimate circle of friends (3:32; Ps. 25:14), or else of the matters discussed in either (Am. 3:7; Ps. 55:14).

11:14. Get all the advice you can
Guidance (RSV) is a fair equivalent to the Heb. word arising from

the tackle of a ship, and hence the handling and steering of it. *Cf.* 1:5, and subject-study: Wisdom, 1(4). Although one can take too many opinions (*cf.* King Zedekiah, Je. 38), it is fatally easy to shut out disquieting voices. The theme recurs in 15:22; 20:18; 24:6.

11:15. Standing surety
See 6:1–5, where this is treated at length; *cf.* 17:18. *Sure* (AV, RV, second line): better, 'carefree'. The word-play in AV, RV is not in the Heb.

11:16. Charm
Ruthlessness is not the only way to the top. That is one point of the proverb, and there is probably a further point implied by the two prizes. Moffatt, by inserting an explanatory 'only', brings out the concealed contrast: 'A charming woman wins respect: high-handed men win only wealth.' As to the kind of charm that is in mind, verse 22 shows that it must go deeper than good looks (*cf.* 31:30).

The verb (the same in both lines) means to grasp or attain, not primarily *retain* (AV, RV).

11:17–19. Reaping the consequences
17. The deed affects the doer most. (*Cf.* 11:29; 12:20.) The principle works itself out in the realm of relationships (Lk. 6:38), character (Is. 58:10, 11) and destiny (Jas. 2:13). The kindness spoken of is *ḥeseḏ*, steadfast love, like God's; and *troubleth* has ominous echoes of the story of Achan (Jos. 7:25, 26), and of the charge which Elijah had to fling back at Ahab (1 Ki. 18:17, 18); see note on 15:6.

18. Only honest achievements satisfy. The Heb. for *work* (AV) can mean also *wages* (RV, RSV); here the second line shows it is the latter. Moffatt puts it vividly: 'It is not real, what a bad man gains.'

19. The end is life or death. The Heb. words for *as* (AV) and for *stedfast* (RV, RSV) are identical in form (*kēn*). Taken either way, the Heb. construction is abrupt. LXX, with some additional support, reads the Heb. *ben*, *i.e.* 'son', which makes a smoother beginning: 'a son of righteousness . . .'. Each of these renderings leaves the main contrast intact.

11:20. Hateful or delightful to God

The basic meaning of *froward* (AV) or *perverse* (RV, RSV) is 'twisted', and the contrast with 'straightforward' in the second line favours Knox's rendering: 'false'.

11:21. Justice will be done

The opening expression is lit. 'hand to hand', probably an allusion to shaking hands on a promise, so meaning 'depend on it' (*cf.* RSV). In the second line, *seed* (AV, RV) will mean more than mere descendants: rather, those who show themselves to be of this breed (*cf.* Jn. 8:39; Gal. 3:7).

11:22. Beauty – and the beast

The proverb puts it more forcibly than we might. Where we (to whom the outward is the impressive part) would have spoken of the lady as a little disappointing, Scripture sees her as a monstrosity. In contrast, see verse 16, where the charm is not skin-deep, and 1 Samuel 25:33, where Abigail is praised for the discretion, or right judgment, which this proverb counts all-important.

11:23. Desire – and fulfilment

The second line gives the clue to what the first (with forceful compression) is concerned with, namely, the outcome, under God's judgment, of what we set our hearts on (*cf.* RSV). See note on 10:24.

11:24–26. The rewards of generosity

24. This verse emphasizes the paradox that you must sometimes lose to gain. It is drawn from the business world, not necessarily from farming (*scattereth* (AV, RV) is a quite general term), and its application is left quite open. But almsgiving is an obvious example (Ps. 112:9; 2 Cor. 9:6–9), and, more deeply, the giving of oneself (Jn. 12:24,25). In the second line, RSV's *withholds what he should give* is safer than AV, RV.

25. This is less paradoxical, approaching the matter along the line of verse 17 (where see note).

26. The verse brings in specifically the heavenly dimension, through the prayers or imprecations that are provoked. Here the withholding (a different word from that of 24) is a calculated act to force up the price – not the mere miserliness of 24.

11:27. What you seek for others, you will get yourself
A single word, suggesting watching for the dawn, underlies the expression *diligently seeks*; see note on 1:28. For the general theme of the proverb, *cf.* verse 17.

11:28. Prosperity – false and true
The first man is precariously propped up; the second has the resilience of life and growth.

RSV alters *fall* (*yippōl*) to *wither* (*yibbōl*), a tempting touch, but without textual support or real necessity.

11:29. It's yourself you are damaging
This is a variation on the theme introduced in verse 17. See also the comment there on the word *troubleth*, which might be translated here 'unsettles'.

11:30. Virtue spreads its blessings
The sense of the Heb. (AV, RV) is that a righteous man has a life-giving influence, and a wise man wins others to wisdom. The phrase 'to win souls (*i.e.* people)' can, however, also mean 'to take lives', when the context demands it (as in 1 Ki. 19:4); and by substituting 'violence' (*ḥāmās*) for 'wise man' (*ḥākām*), the LXX provides such a context, and is followed by RSV. But the Old Testament knows the metaphor of capturing people with ideas or influences (*cf.* in a bad sense, 6:25; 2 Sa. 15:6); and the promise, 'thou shalt catch men', was doubly apt if it was meant to awaken echoes of this proverb.

11:31. Strict requital

Requited (RSV) can have a reassuring or a threatening ring; the LXX makes it the latter, and is supported by being quoted in full in 1 Peter 4:18 ('if the righteous scarcely be saved . . .'). In other words, nobody sins with impunity; not even a Moses or a David, much less the confirmed rebel (*cf.* Je. 25:29; Ezk. 18:24). It is important to notice that in 1 Peter 4:12–19 even the suffering of the righteous under persecution is partly viewed (as in this proverb) as a judgment, whatever other aspects it wears.

12:1. Welcome discipline

If you think yourself above criticism, you are not worth it. *Cf.* verse 15.

12:2. God loves kindness

Platitude? But every religious man needs the reminder; *cf.* 1 John 4:8.

12:3. No righteousness, no roots

Cf. 10:25.

12:4. A fine wife

The modern sense of *virtuous* (AV, RV) does no justice to the Heb. term's root idea of strength and worth (see note on 31:10, and *cf.* the full-length portrait in the ensuing verses there). The modern phrase, 'she has a lot in her', expresses something of the meaning.

12:5. As the man, so the policy

Thoughts mean primarily 'intentions', 'plans'. Moffatt puts it well: 'The aims of a good man are honourable: the plans of a bad man are underhand.' If this is a truism, it is one which is overlooked whenever leaders are elected on the strength of their promises rather than their principles.

12:6. Words lethal or liberating

The literal sense is best: *i.e.* '. . . are a lying-in-wait for blood'; in

other words, '. . . are an ambush'. The second line ends, lit.,
'. . . delivers them' (*i.e.* the upright themselves), and in this
answer to the first line there may be a glance at the thought of
1:18, that your trap tends to trap *you*. Alternatively the point
may be that sincerity is the best defence against slander.

12:7. Time is the test
This is perhaps best read (as RVmg): *Overthrow the wicked, and
they are not.* Another assurance of the inherent instability of evil.
Cf. 10:25; 12:3.

12:8. Good sense wins respect
The *wisdom* (AV, RV) that is in mind here is the kind that Abigail
displayed (*śekel*, 1 Sa. 25:3; *cf.* subject-study: Wisdom, I(3));
and the contrasted quality in the second line suggests inability
to think straight. Toy proposes, excellently, 'wrongheaded'.

12:9. Threadbare gentility
It is a tilt at the odd valuations we make. As the Heb. text stands
(see AV, RV), *better* means 'better-off', 'more enviable'. But RSV,
following LXX, Syr., reads the same Heb. consonants to mean:
*Better is a man of humble standing who works for himself than one who
plays the great man but lacks bread.* This is stronger, and gives more
content to the word 'better'.

12:10. Kindness, even to animals
Why is the righteous man considerate? Partly because by
definition he respects the due relations and proportions of things
(whereas the wicked man considers only himself); but chiefly
because he is a man of God, instructed in God's ways (*cf.* Ex.
23:12; Jon. 4:11) and himself a recipient of mercy. Besides
emphasizing this important aspect of the biblical meaning of
righteousness, this proverb illustrates the warm, personal
quality of the Heb. verb 'to know', which is the verb translated
regardeth in the first line.

12:11. Frivolity fills no cupboards
Vain persons (AV, RV) could equally be 'vain things' (RSV: *worth-*

less pursuits). Either way, opportunities of solid achievement are being busily frittered away (the Heb. for *followeth* is intensive here; this man lacks discrimination, not energy). The proverb is perhaps specially relevant to the temptations of the present age of quick travel and packaged entertainment. A fully symmetrical version of the saying is found at 28:19.

12:12. The fascination of the forbidden
The second line brings an abrupt change of metaphor, hence the conjectural emendations of, *e.g.*, RSV. The text as it stands appears to contrast the delusive attractions of evil methods with the quiet rewards of goodness. But line 1 may possibly refer to the judgment awaiting the wicked, to which they unwittingly hasten: *cf.* 1:17,18.

12:13,14. Words and deeds come back to roost
13. *Cf.* Matthew 12:36,37. For better or worse, your words give you away.

14. Words can bring in as substantial a return as deeds, for they establish relationships and implant ideas. (See subject-study: Words, pp. 46ff.)

12:15. The man who is never wrong
We show ourselves men of reason when we *listen* (RSV) to reason, and test ourselves for prejudice. The person who always knows best may be the only one unconscious of his real name.

12:16. Self-control is sense
RSV rightly follows Moffatt's second line: *the prudent man ignores an insult.* (*Cf.* 9:7a for this meaning of AV, RV's *shame.*) The verb in this line is that of 10:12b, where a similar reticence has a still better motive.

12:17–19. Words good and bad
See subject-study: Words, pp. 46ff.
17. Words are an outcrop of character. So it is the man who is *habitually* truthful who will give proper evidence in a

crisis. (Moffatt's, 'A man who gives true evidence furthers justice', is a little strained, however important its insistence on impartiality.) Knox has, excellently, 'Nothing but his honest thought a lover of truth declares, a false witness nothing but lies.'

18. The deep thrust of words. The verb in the first line contains the idea of rashness (almost 'blurt out'), which AV misses. It is used of Moses' outburst, in Psalm 106:33. Moffatt brings out the contrast of the second line well: 'but there is healing power in thoughtful words'.

19. Only truth has permanence – and only the true. *Cf.* 19:5, and note.

12:20. The plans you shape, shape you
Joy is an unexpected alternative to *deceit*; the two halves of the proverb make the point that what we pursue for others, and the way we pursue it, leaves its mark on our cast of mind. *Peace* (AV, RV) includes the idea of general welfare – and to be planning this for other people is to enjoy its by-products ourselves.

12:21. More than conquerors
The verb used for *happen* (AV, RV; *cf.* Ps. 91:10) suggests being sent or allowed. The rigid application of this law was the mainstay of Job's comforters; but taken rightly, it is a stimulating truth, as valid for Paul (Rom. 8:28 with 36,37) as for Joseph (Gn. 50:20) – cheaply held in prosperity, precious in adversity.

12:22. Another thing God detests
Cf. verse 19, for which this verse supplies the ultimate foundation.

12:23. Discretion
There is an extra punch in the final word. The simple contrast would lie between the ability and inability to keep quiet; but the fool gives *himself* away, as well as his secret.

12:24. Laziness has its price
Tribute (AV), or better, *forced labour* (RSV), was a subject on

which Solomon was all too qualified to pronounce; and he spoke more truly than he could have guessed on the reward of diligence: see 1 Kings 11:28ff.

12:25. Anxiety

This word, rather than AV, RV's *heaviness*, gives the normal sense of the Heb.; *cf.* Joshua 22:24. *A good word* is wider than the good news which would remove the cause of the anxiety but is not always possible; a good word gives courage to face it. *Cf.* 18:14.

12:26. Walk circumspectly

The translators differ greatly on the first line. AV is possible but unlikely; RSV emends freely; RV (*is a guide to his neighbour*) takes the most probable verb (to investigate, make reconnaissance: *cf.* Dt. 1:33; Ec. 7:25), but inserts a preposition. Delitzsch revocalizes *neighbour*, to read 'pasture'. Yet the literal translation is not meaningless: 'makes investigation of his close friend' (Heb. *mērēa'* as in 19:7; Jdg. 15:2). That is to say, he does not rush into a friendship, and does not surrender his moral judgment to anyone. The need of such reconnaissance is made plain by the second line.

12:27. Fleeting opportunity

The translation *roasteth* (AV, RV) is a guess, founded on Jewish tradition and on Arabic and Aramaic roots meaning to scorch. Another guess, based on another Arabic root, is 'starteth not his quarry' (the phrase *that which he took in hunting* (AV, RV) is in Heb. a single word). RSV, following LXX, uses the verb *catch*. In each case, whether as non-finisher or non-starter, the indolent man throws away his chances.

The second line in AV (*but the substance of a diligent man is precious*) yields an excellent contrast, but it assumes that two Heb. words have changed places. (The Heb. as it stands reads: 'but the substance of a precious man is diligent'.) This assumption by AV is as small and as rewarding as any that have been put forward for this unusual line. An alternative, which involves no alterations, is 'But a rare treasure of a man is one who is diligent' (Bertholet, Ewald, cited by Toy), which is intelligible but inapposite.

12:28. The way of life

While the first line puts the point of the proverb beyond doubt, the Heb. of the second defies translation as it stands. The following two suggestions demand (unlike RSV) no change in the consonantal text:

(a) 'And the journey of her pathway is no-death!' (BDB, p. 667a, *s.v. nāṯîḇ*; *cf. op. cit.*, p. 39a, *s.v.* '*al*, b., c.)

(b) 'But [there is] a way [which is] a path to (*'el*) death' (W. J. Martin, orally).

The second of these is the smoother construction; it also fits the prevailing pattern of antitheses. But the first is closer to the existing text, and has had fresh support claimed for it from Ugaritic.[1]

On the meaning of *life* and *death*, see subject-study, pp. 53ff.

13:1. Teachability

The pairing of a *son*, under training, with a *scorner*, who is a fool in the last stages of folly (*cf.* 26:12), suggests that if you cannot stand home truths from your own father you are well on the way to becoming insufferable.

13:2, 3. Words fruitful or fatal

2. Words pass; their fruit remains. Perhaps *soul* (AV, RV) here means appetite (see note on 10:3); hence RSV: *the desire of the treacherous is for violence*. But AV, RV give a more direct counterpart to the statement in the first line, that words bring a tangible return. In the second line, AV's *transgressors* should be *treacherous* (RV, RSV).

---

[1] M. Dahood (*Biblica*, 1960, pp. 176-181) considers that '*l mwt* ('no-death!') here corresponds to *bl mt* (no death) in Anath's offer of immortality to Aqhat (see AQHT A vi 25-32, in *ANET*, p.151b); *cf.* 'no-dew! and no-rain!' in 2 Sa. 1:21 and AQHT C i 42-46, *ANET*, p.153b. He therefore finds immortality promised here.

3. Ammunition for your enemy. This rashness could show itself in promises, assertions, disclosures; the ruin could be financial, social, physical, spiritual.

13:4. Sloth leaves you dissatisfied
See subject-study: The Sluggard, 1, pp. 42f.

13:5. Words fair and foul
The translation of the second line, which determines the main point of the saying, turns on whether we take the two verbs in their primary or their secondary senses. *Prima facie* they mean 'causes to stink and makes ashamed'; they can however mean *acts shamefully and disgracefully* (RSV; *cf*. AV, RV). Though it is a minority view, the former seems preferable, as giving a more specific antithesis to line 1; the proverb as a whole contrasting a scrupulous fairness with a readiness to 'smear' and slander.

13:6. Honesty is safety
Cf. 11:3-9.

13:7, 8. Riches and poverty
   7. Don't take a man at his own valuation. It is a proverb of detached observation, leaving the reader to draw his own conclusions. Together with the next verse, it is a reminder that, both subjectively and objectively, money is but a small ingredient of wealth or poverty. Judging by 12:9b, where the verb is in a similar state, we should probably translate (with most modern versions): '. . . that plays the rich man, . . . the poor man'. On the other hand, the meaning . . . *maketh himself rich*, . . . *poor* (AV, RV) is possible, with implications as in Luke 12:21; 2 Corinthians 6:10. *Cf.* Proverbs 11:24. (The ambiguity of this verbal voice is well illustrated in 2 Samuel 13, where Amnon makes himself ill (2) and feigns illness (5, 6) in identical terms.)
   8. Poverty has its compensations. RV substitutes *threatening* (*cf.* Is. 30:17) for AV's *rebuke*, and Moffatt puts it neatly: 'A rich man may buy off his life: a poor man can ignore the

robber's threat.' (RSV makes an unsupported 'correction' in the second line.) The two extremes, in fact, may meet, and not only in the presence of gangsters. The rich man may spend his fortune meeting his commitments (*cf.* Ec. 5:11) and avoiding fears to which a poor man offers too small a target.

13:9. Bright prospect
Rejoiceth is (in spite of criticisms, and of the LXX's variant: 'is for ever') a natural and lively simile; *cf.* our 'burning merrily'. The proverb refers to the life and expectations of the two kinds of men (*cf.* Ps. 18:28; Jb. 18:5,6; 21:17); a different use is made of the idea in 20:27 and Matthew 6:22,23. The phrase *be put out* should rather be 'go out'. Delitzsch draws a telling contrast between daylight and rushlight; but while the Heb. words allow this they do not require it (Je. 25:10, Heb.), and both terms are used of the wicked man in Job 18:6.

13:10. The products of pride
For the word used here for *pride* (AV, RV), see note on 11:2. It is stated to be an ingredient in every quarrel; not, that is, in every difference of opinion, but in the clash of competing and un-yielding personalities. *Those who take advice* (RSV) show up, by contrast, the closed minds which are another symptom of pride.

13:11. Easy come, easy go
RSV and Moffatt adopt the LXX and Vulg. reading (strengthened by 20:21) of 'in haste', for *by vanity*, which represents the transposition of two Heb. letters. The implied sense remains the same; and the saying, rooted in the facts of character, is plentifully exemplified by gamblers. *Increase* (AV, RV) should be *increase it* (RSV), *i.e.* wealth. See the note on 20:21.

13:12. Hope deferred
Deferred does not imply a revising of what was promised, but literally, something 'long drawn out'. It is a help to recognize (and so guard against the natural reaction to) the slow maturing of God's harvest (Jas. 5:7). The second line matches the first,

more closely than in AV, RV, with another participle: lit., 'desire come', hence RSV *a desire fulfilled.* On *tree of life, cf.* 3:18; 11:30; and subject-study: Life and Death, p. 54. Here it is used purely psychologically, of the reviving of drooping spirits.

13:13. Obedience pays

Word and *commandment* are a reminder that *revealed* religion is presupposed in Proverbs.

13:14. Law means life

If the mixture of metaphors is harsh to our ears, the sense is clear, and the ideas of refreshment and safe guidance are most apt. The phrase *law of the wise* (man) (AV, RV) indicates that *law* (*tôrâ*) is here used in its original sense of 'direction' or 'instruction' (see note on 3:1); it is the voice of spiritual experience rather than divine command, though it will be in harmony with *the* Torah (as its proximity to verse 13 emphasizes).

13:15. Tact with integrity

On RSV's *good sense* (*śekel ṭôḇ*) see subject-study: Wisdom, I (3). The AV of the second line is famous, but needs modifying. *Transgressors* should be *the treacherous* (RV); and *hard* is not easily justified. The Heb. word (*'êṯān*) normally means 'perennial', chiefly as applied to the flow of a river, but also to, *e.g.*, the permanence of a rock (Nu. 24:21). It is very doubtful whether *hard* (RV: *rugged*) is a legitimate extension of this; its only support comes from the AV of Deuteronomy 21:4 ('rough valley'), but the identical phrase in Amos 5:24 clearly means 'perennial stream'. It therefore seems that the Heb. has been miscopied; the LXX suggests that the true Heb. reading was *'êḏām*: 'their destruction'; G. R. Driver[1] more simply still submits that the word *'ê* ('not') has dropped out before the identical first syllable of *'êṯān*, by the common slip of the pen known as haplography, and that the line should end: 'is not lasting'. This seems the best solution.

---

[1] *Biblica*, 1951, p. 181.

13:16. The product proclaims the man

These two types are compared in 12:23 and 15:2, but in a different respect. There, reserve is contrasted with the lack of it; here, character (whether one would hide it or not) is shown to be written all over one's conduct. (RSV, with some versional support, has *in everything a*, for *every*; this is possible, with the change of only a vowel.)

13:17. Envoys good and bad

On the analogy of the second line we should probably construe the first verb of the proverb causatively (leaving the Heb. consonants intact) as in RSV: . . . *plunges men into trouble*. See also 25:13; 26:6.

13:18. Welcome criticism

Cf. the extended treatment of this theme in 1:20–33.

13:19. Heart's desire

The lesson of the proverb is that to set your heart on a thing is to weaken the power to assess it. It must be had, at all costs, not now because of its worth but because you have promised it to yourself. The first line applies, with any permanence, only to a worth-while object: compare Isaiah 53:11 with Psalm 106:15; Ecclesiastes 2:10,11.

13:20. Education by friendship

The second line overleaps the expected climax (which Knox, translating the Vulg., raps out as 'Fool he ends that fool befriends') into the disaster that lies on the far side of folly. As to the nature of this, the Heb. allows a choice between 'shall become evil' and (as in 11:15) 'shall suffer evil'.[1]

13:21,22. Requital

Notice the general (21, AV, RV) and the ethical (22) senses of *good*, side by side. As elsewhere in Proverbs, the promised

---

[1] *Cf. Ahikar*, IV, *DOTT*, p. 271.

requital is implied to be the outworking of the various qualities that make up the good or bad man; but not without God. Proverbs is concerned with the general rule; Job (*e.g.* chapter 21) with the exceptions.

13:23. Method matters most
The point of this very terse proverb seems to be that the size of your resources matters less than the judgment with which you handle them. AV concludes: *but there is that is destroyed for want of judgment*, using this last word in the sense found in Isaiah 28:26 (AV: 'discretion'), in a similar context of good husbandry. (The inconsistency between the poor man's *fallow ground* (RSV, rather than *tillage*, AV, RV) and the stated abundance, disappears on this reading of the proverb, which is concerned with its potentialities.)

13:24. Spare the rod, spoil the child
This is not a purely Old Testament attitude: it is expounded more fully in Hebrews 12:5-11. The latter passage draws attention to the imperfect motives of human fathers, and Ephesians 6:4 warns against undue severity; but the obligation remains. Proverbs itself exalts the place of tenderness, constructiveness and example, in this relationship: see, *e.g.*, 4:3,4, 11. (*Betimes*, AV, RV: the phrase is lit. 'he seeks him early (or, earnestly) with discipline': see note on 1:28.) See also subject-study: The Family, pp. 50f.

13:25. Requital
It is a proverb not on moderation but on retribution: see note on verses 21, 22. AV, RV *soul* here means *appetite* (RSV); *cf.* 10:3, and note.

14:1. The home-maker
The Heb. consonants of *wise* and *buildeth* (AV, RV) are identical with those of the opening words of 9:1. Probably we should read therefore 'Womanly wisdom buildeth' (lit., 'wisdom of women . . .'); especially since *the foolish* is here the abstract word

folly (RSV). The sense remains much as in AV, RV, but with more stress on the qualities (as against the bare choice) on which the fortunes of a home depend. (RSV takes the liberty of omitting the Heb. word 'women'.) See also subject-study: The Family, p. 50.

14:2. Not only with our lips
The 'despising' may be unconscious, but none the less real. Every departure from God's path is a pitting of one's will, and a backing of one's judgment, against His; but the contempt which it spells is too irrational to acknowledge.

14:3. Words come back to roost
This word *rod*, or 'sprig', occurs elsewhere only in Isaiah 11:1; hence it may indicate something which reveals the hidden root's vitality, so that the fool is giving himself away. But a better contrast with the second line is given if the word can mean a *punitive* rod (which is not certain); *i.e.*, a rod for his pride. (RSV's emendation, *a rod for his back* – cf. 10:13; 26:3 – is attractive, but involves an unsupported though small change of consonants as well as vowels.)

14:4. Neat but negative
Orderliness can reach the point of sterility. This proverb is not a plea for slovenliness, physical or moral, but for the readiness to accept upheaval, and a mess to clear up, as the price of growth. It has many applications to personal, institutional and spiritual life, and could well be inscribed in the minute-books of religious bodies, to foster a farmer's outlook, rather than a curator's.

14:5. Witnesses true and false
See 12:17, and note. Other proverbs on the subject may be found at 6:19; 14:25; 19:5,9; 21:28; 24:28; 25:18.

14:6. Wisdom eludes the know-all
From this verse the scoffer emerges as one who is not purely flippant; he may be a keen thinker: it is only (but fatally) his refusal of God that gives him his name. The motto of the book

(1:7) explains his failure and the success of his opposite (*cf.* Jb. 28:28; 1 Jn. 2:27).

14:7. Empty encounter

The Heb. is elusive; it may be hypothetical ('if you go . . .'), as RV takes it to be (though RV's 'into' is a little unlikely); or, more probably, it is a command: 'Go from . . ., for . . .'. Moffatt puts the conclusion forcibly: 'You will not find a word of sense in him.' See subject-study: The Fool, II (1), p. 40.

14:8. Real sense and real folly

Way in Proverbs means 'conduct' rather than 'career': hence this saying makes moral reflection the essence of shrewdness, whereas we tend to reduce shrewdness to business-sense. Likewise the essence of folly is mental dishonesty: not merely falling short of the truth (as we must), but side-stepping it. The next proverb presses this home.

14:9. Moral insolence

Two translations are possible. (a) As the verb is singular, it suggests the rendering: '(The) guilt (-offering) scorns fools' – *i.e.* sacrifice is unavailing for the thoughtless (*cf.* 21:27). The word *favour* (AV, RSV) in the second line, which is used in sacrificial contexts to denote divine acceptance, lends some support to this; but the imagery seems far-fetched, and the second line is speaking of relations *among* (not towards) men. RSV adopts this general sense, but makes drastic 'correction' of the Heb. text. (b) The singular verb can in Heb. be harnessed to a plural subject, to express the sense 'every one of them'; and this yields the excellent meaning: 'Every fool mocks at guilt' (*cf.* AV, RV). With the second line, the whole proverb contrasts the unconcern of fools for the damage they do, Godward and manward,[1] with the care of the upright to preserve goodwill.

14:10. The inmost heart

Other aspects of the solitariness of each man are seen in verse 14,

---

[1] See Lv. 6:1-7 for the dual reference, vertical and horizontal, of *'āšām*, guilt (-offering).

and 9:12. The word *stranger* possibly implies that to a friend this impassable door might open; but more probably it only signifies 'another', as in Job 19:27b (to which Oesterley draws attention).

14:11. Retribution
On this theme, see note on 10:2, 3.

Flourish is an energetic word in Heb., suggesting a tree bursting into bud.

14:12. The false trail
Right means 'straight' or 'level': it is often a moral term, as in the previous verse ('upright'), but here it is a seeming short cut to success, taken by those who are impatient of advice (*cf.* 12:15), or of hard work (*cf.* 15:19), or of moral scruples (*cf.* 13:14). The proverb is repeated exactly at 16:25.

14:13. Bitter-sweet gaiety
The AV, by inserting *that* (*the end of that mirth*), unduly limits the second line. One of two meanings seems likely: (a) there is tragedy in life, from which gaiety offers no full or final escape (*cf.* Lk. 6:21, 25; Jn. 16:20–22); (b) our moods are seldom untinged with their opposites, and are none of them permanent.

14:14. Table for one
Strikingly contrasted testimonies to the two halves of this saying are given by the two Sauls (1 Sa. 26:21b; 2 Tim. 4:7). RSV's emendation is unnecessary, and weakens the close. Other glimpses of human loneliness are found in verses 10 and 13, and in 9:12.

14:15–17. Examples of folly and sense
There are different ways of being a fool. We may be (a) gullible (15), taking on hearsay what we should verify for ourselves; (b) over-confident (16), like Peter before Gethsemane, or Amaziah with Joash (2 Ch. 25:17ff.), playing with fire; (c) irascible (17a), acting on the state of our feelings, not the merits of the

case: *cf.* verse 29, which emphasizes that to see a situation calmly is to see it clearly. (In 17b, the Heb. text (AV, RV) shows that the cold cunning of 'a man of schemes' may be even worse to live with than a hot temper. RSV needlessly follows the LXX here, which ends with a favourable verb ('is patient') and therefore interprets the 'schemes' favourably – as indeed one can, if the context demands it. But RSV's too-brief footnote implies, unwarrantably, that the Heb. text is nonsense.)

14:18. The fool and the wise rewarded
This is forward-looking. RSV's *acquire* is clearer than AV, RV *inherit*, for the proverb is not blaming a man's folly on his heredity, but warning him that by habituation he is storing up only more and more foolishness, till, as in 24, it will be the only thing he has.

14:19. Evil pays homage
Goodness, however scant its earnings, commonly wins a reluctant or unconscious respect (*cf.* the definition of hypocrisy as the homage which vice pays to virtue). The Old Testament in its own terms, and the New Testament in fuller detail, promise complete vindication; the perfect tense of the Heb., as often used in prophetic oracles, expresses the certainty of it.

14:20. Fair-weather friends
See subject-study: The Friend, p. 45, for similar as well as counterbalancing statements. See also the next verse, for a moral judgment.

14:21. The sin of contempt
The many angles from which Proverbs observes a matter can be seen in its treatment of unkindness. In verse 20 it is drily reported – this is how things are. In 11:12, it is seen as the negation of sense. Here, to go deeper, it is shown to be a rejection of the will and (line 2) the blessing of God. On rich and poor, see references given at verse 31.

14:22. Paid in their own coin

Err, or 'go astray', refers to their misguided policy (*cf.* the second line); their morals need no comment. Moffatt gives the ending compellingly: 'Good-natured men find people kind and true.'

14:23. Toil or talk

See subject-study: Words, p. 47.

The same Heb. terms for *profit* and *penury* (*want*, RSV) recur in 21:5.

14:24. Crown or fool's cap

RSV has some support for assuming two fairly small miscopyings, and reading: *The crown of the wise is their wisdom, but folly is the garland of fools*. But the Heb. text (AV, RV) is meaningful: the first line agrees with, *e.g.*, 8:18, and the second emphasizes by its very tautology the barrenness of folly, which is its own reproach and its own harvest (see note on verse 18).

14:25. Unyielding honesty

The special Christian overtones of the first line in AV, RV do not really belong to it: the context (unlike that of 11:30) is the law-court, and *souls* are 'people' or *lives* (RSV). The second line is more exactly rendered: 'and one who breathes out lies is deceit'. A man who will trim the facts for you will trim them as easily against you; and a career or a life may hang on a word. See note on 12:17, and references at 14:5.

14:26,27. Godliness – fortress and fountain

Godliness protects the soul by its solidity (26) and its vitality (27). Both aspects are necessary, since evil not only attacks but attracts us; therefore the man of God must know (and show his family, 26b) something both stronger and better (*cf.* also 13:14). *His* children could mean 'God's' (*cf.* Dt. 14:1), but the expression is rare in the Old Testament, and most commentators connect it with the godly man implied in 26a. (In RSV, 'his' is American idiom for 'one's'.)

14:28. A king's glory
It is a reminder that solitary splendour is self-extinguishing. The true leader glories in the vigour of his followers.

14:29,30. Live peaceably
29. The wisdom of it. The converse of the first line is 17a, where see comment. *Exalteth* means either 'displays to public view' or 'promotes'. *Cf.* 3:35; but there the person is the object.

30. The boon of it. For *sound*, RSV has *tranquil*, which makes a good antithesis to the *envy* (AV, RV) or *passion* (RSV) of the second line. But the Heb. term is general. *Heart* is figurative (RSV: *mind*), and the proverb teaches that to nurse a resentment is bad for body as well as soul: it is no sacrifice when we renounce it. *Cf.* 17:22.

14:31. Rags and respect
The best comment is Job 31:15, which argues likewise from God's Creatorship. Other considerations are added in James 2:5 (God's choice), Matthew 25:40 (Christ's manhood), 1 John 3:17,18 (the Christian's sincerity). See also verses 20, 21; 17:5; 19:17; 22:2; 28:8; 29:13.

14:32. Final ruin or final refuge
RSV, following LXX and Syr., emends *death* to *integrity*; a far-reaching change. This yields closer parallelism and easier sense; it assumes a copyist's transposition of two consonants. The Heb. text, however (AV, RV), must not be discarded merely as implying too advanced a doctrine of death: Job and the Psalms show occasional glimpses, such as this, of what lies normally beyond their view; in any case (as Delitzsch points out) the righteous man commits himself to God in death (Ps. 31:5), whatever the state of his knowledge. Whichever reading is adopted, *finds refuge* (RSV) should be 'seeks refuge'; *cf.* AV, RV, *hath hope*.

14:33. Where wisdom is at home
Two meanings of the Heb. text are possible. (a)A wise man

does not parade his knowledge; a fool does (*cf.* 12:23). (b)While wisdom's true abode is with the wise, even among fools it is not wholly unrecognized.

14:34. A nation's stature

Here is the most searching test of policies and achievements; *cf.* 16:12b. Uncompromising as it is, it is fully realistic: *cf.* Amos 1 and 2, and the sequel in history. *Exalteth* is not a material but a moral term here, as its converse shows. *Reproach*, or 'disgrace', is a strong word found elsewhere only in Leviticus 20:17 (AV: 'a wicked thing').

14:35. Efficiency rewarded

The saying is a bracing reminder not to blame luck or favouritism but one's own shortcomings, for any lack of recognition. Moffatt gives the sense well: 'The king favours an able minister; his anger is for the incompetent.' *Cf.* 22:29.

15:1. A soft answer

For related passages, see subject-study: Words, III, p. 48.

A harsh word (RSV) is rightly singular (as against AV): a single word that hurts (the Heb. implies this) is enough to 'make anger rise up'.

15:2. Responsible utterance

Useth ... aright (AV) is best. It is a single word, meaning basically to do a thing well (*cf.* 30:29, 'walk finely'; Ezk. 33:32, 'play skilfully'), RSV (*dispenses*) and Moffatt ('distils') gratuitously change the Heb. to secure a neater contrast with the second line. But the question here is not 'Much talk or little?', but 'Considered or unconsidered?'; *cf.* verse 28 .

15:3. The eyes of the Lord

The equally striking 2 Chronicles 16:9 brings out God's saving purpose in this. Our present verse shows the range and persistence of this scrutiny; verse 11 its penetration; verses 8, 9 its sensitivity.

15:4. Words: life-giving, death-dealing

Wholesome (AV, RV) is preferable to RSV's *gentle*, which unduly limits the scope of the root idea of 'healing' (*cf.* 'remedy', 6:15, AV, RV; and note there the contrasted 'broken', as in our second line). *Perverseness* (*seleph*) is a quality of the treacherous in 11:3 (AV, RV), and implies what is twisted, or false. The nearly identical Heb. expression in Isaiah 65:14 for *a breaking of the spirit* (RV) suggests that the effect of words on 'morale' (*cf.* 13:12) is chiefly in mind here, though it can be taken further.

15:5. Impatience of criticism

Cf. 13:1,18, and subject-study: Wisdom, II (2), p. 38. In the second line, the last verb can mean either *is prudent* (AV, RSV) or, 'becomes prudent' (*cf.* RV). The Heb. of 1 Samuel 23:22 justifies the former, which makes a sharp antithesis to the knowingness of the fool; but Proverbs 19:25 shows that the latter translation is equally tenable.

15:6. What are you storing up?

The root for *trouble* is mostly used in situations where one man brings calamity on many. Achan's name resembles it, and is made to coincide with it in 1 Chronicles 2:7. His story in Joshua 7 makes a good background to the second line of the proverb, and Genesis 14:22–15:1 to the first line. *Cf.* also verse 27, and note on 11:17.

15:7. What are you spreading?

Note the unexpected collation of *heart* (RSV: 'minds') with *lips*, to make the point that if you take care of your outlook, your influence will take care of itself. *Cf.* 4:23.

15:8, 9. Divine disgust, divine delight

The pair of sayings show how intensely our regular behaviour matters to God (*cf.* verse 3). In verse 8, *sacrifice* and *prayer* may be intended as parallel activities; but the fact that sacrifice is the more 'full-dress' approach helps to sharpen the point of the saying. *Cf.* verse 29; 21:3, 27; 28:9; and the prophets, from

Samuel (1 Sa. 15:22) onwards. In verse 9, the word *followeth* is in the intensive voice of the verb, implying that a strong purposefulness is God's special joy.

15:10. Life-saving reproof
Most modern versions construe this as RV: *There is grievous correction . . .*, with the implied progression: 'To be wayward is asking for a lesson; to be unteachable is asking for death.' The AV is equally possible, and perhaps preferable (*Correction is grievous . . .*); it implies that the first state threatens to harden into the second, since those who most need criticism are most impatient of it, and most in danger. *Cf.* verses 5, 12, and subject-study: Life and Death, p. 56.

15:11. Naked and open
In some moods, Old Testament writers could think of *Sheol* (the realm of the dead; AV, misleadingly, *hell*) as beyond God's sight and memory (*e.g.* Ps. 88); and they could use similar terms for their own contemporary plight (*e.g.* Ps. 44:24). But if that is how they felt, they also knew better; and this verse has its parallels in, *e.g.*, Job 26:6; Psalm 139:8; Amos 9:2. *Abaddon* (AV: *destruction*) is either a synonym for Sheol, emphasizing state as against place, or a term for its 'uttermost parts' (Is. 14:15, RV), reserved for the most wicked. Sheol and Abaddon are coupled again in 27:20; Job 26:6; and Abaddon is a title of the devil in Revelation 9:11.

15:12. Speak to us smooth things
To be reproved (RV, RSV) is correct; not 'a reprover' (*cf.* AV). The scoffer is not as fearless as he pretends. *Cf.* Ahab and Micaiah, 1 Kings 22:8.

15:13. Morale
The *heart* stands for the thoughts and attitude; and these, not the circumstances, are decisive. Knox: 'Gay heart, gay looks; sad thoughts crush the spirit.' *Cf.* verse 15; 17:22; 18:14.

15:14. Seeker and trifler
The ill-matched verbs give an edge to the contrast: the purpose-fulness of *seeketh*, and the random nibbling of *feedeth* (the Heb. verb denotes the grazing of cattle); and the pairing of the nouns also repays study. For an application, see the comment on 12:11.

15:15. Morale
If verse 13 shows that our prevailing attitude colours our whole personality, this saying makes it also colour our whole experience. *Cf.* Genesis 47:9 with 2 Timothy 4:6–8; or Ruth 1:20,21 with Habakkuk 3:17,18.

15:16, 17. Priorities, spiritual and temporal
   16. *Trouble* is a less disastrous word than that of 15:6; Moffatt's 'wealth with worry' is perfect (contrast 'godliness with content-ment', 1 Tim. 6:6). See further on 16:8.
   17. *Cf.* 17:1.

15:18. Storm-centre
The point here is that quarrels depend on *people* far more than on subject-matter; *cf.*, with the second line, R. T. Archibald's characterization of the 'peacemakers' in the Beatitude: '. . . who carry about with them an atmosphere in which quarrels die a natural death'. (*Strife . . . strife*: the Heb. is not guilty of the repetition in AV; better, RSV's *strife . . . contention*.) See also verse 1, and 29:22.

15:19. The lazy take the most trouble
The sluggard is contrasted, a little unexpectedly, with the upright or straightforward – a reminder (a) that there is an element of dishonesty in laziness (trying to sidestep the facts and one's share of the load); (b) that the straight course is ultimately the easiest. *Cf.* 4:25,26; also subject-study: The Sluggard, p. 43.

15:20. '. . . Bound up in the lad's life'
See note on the similar 10:1. The second line breaks fresh

ground by leaving the mother's grief to be inferred, and stating instead the callousness of one who is fool enough (lit., 'a fool of a man') to inflict it.

15:21. The playboy
This saying brings out the element of choice in the career of the fool. The feckless man (the term used in 12:11; *cf.* Ho. 7:11) follows his fancy; the man of discernment is concerned to set a straight course (*walketh uprightly* (AV) is akin to 'look straight before thee' in 4:25); *cf.* verse 19.

15:22. Get all the advice you can
See 11:14 and note.

15:23. Verbal craftsmanship
See subject-study: Words, III, p. 48.

15:24. Few there be that find it
RSV is best here: *The wise man's path leads upward to life, that he may avoid Sheol beneath.* For fuller treatment of the two ways in Proverbs, see chapter 2, especially 10–22; also 4:18,19. AV's *hell* = Sheol; see subject-study: Life and Death, p. 55.

15:25. Protector of the poor
The same word for *proud* in 16:19 suggests that these are the highhanded, and the widow is their natural prey. *House* and *border* (RSV: 'boundaries') are effectively contrasted. The story of Naboth (1 Ki. 21) illuminates the saying; but it is relevant to all kinds of exploitation.

15:26. Troublemaking and peacemaking
The second line has its meaning brought out in RSV: *the words of the pure are pleasing to him* (*i.e.* the Lord). *Thoughts* (AV, RSV), in the first line, mean 'plans', and the contrasted language of the second line emphasizes the fact that such plans are hateful to God even before they issue in words or deeds.

15:27. Root of all evil
Gifts (mattānōt: see note on 18:16), like *gain,* can be innocent, but carry great danger. Deranging a man's scale of values (Ec. 7:7), they threaten his home (on *troubleth,* see note on verse 6) and his own soul (contrast the expression *shall live,* and see subject-study: Life and Death, p. 53), and dethrone his God (Eph. 5:5).

15:28. Responsible utterance
This, by its likeness to verse 2, shows how closely wisdom and righteousness agree. *Studieth* (AV, RV) has the idea of musing, meditating (Ps. 63:6); but 24:2 depicts wickedness in an equally painstaking mood.

15:29. God, aloof or at hand
Cf. verse 8 and note.

15:30. A tonic
The light of the eyes may perhaps refer to the radiant face of a friend (*cf.* 16:15); if so, the two lines of the proverb will be speaking of the heartwarming effect that persons and facts, respectively, can bring; *cf.* verse 13; 17:22; 25:25; also Gn. 45:27, 28; Is. 52:7,8.

15:31-33. Three proverbs on teachability
Wisdom repays all the rigours it prescribes; for admittedly its schooling is unflattering (*reproof* (AV, RV), 31,32b) and arduous ('discipline' 32a). The point is made in different ways: 31a commends the process as life-giving; 31b as fitting one for the company of the wise; 32 punctures complacency by showing *whom* the unteachable person, paradoxically, is despising; and 33 puts the matter in perspective by varying the motto of the book (*cf.* 1:7) to show that the fear of the Lord is not merely the gateway but the whole path of wisdom (*instruction of =* 'training in').

16:1-9. The sovereignty of the Lord
  1. Man proposes, God disposes. AV distorts the Heb.,

in which man and God stand in contrast ('Belonging to man
... but from the Lord ...'). So RSV: *The plans of the mind belong to
man. Plans*, or *preparations* (AV, RV), is a word suggesting placing
things in order: *e.g.* setting a battle-array (Gn. 14:8), or laying a
fire (Gn. 22:9).

The meaning of the proverb is probably akin to that of verse
9, but with an emphasis on the fact that for all his freedom to
plan, man only, in the event, advances God's designs. *Cf.* 1
Kings 12:24: 'this thing is from me.'

Cf., with verse 9, 19:21; 20:24; 21:30,31.

2. Weighed in the balances. 21:2 is almost identical, but
12:15a has an illuminating difference.

3. God's safe hands. Our activities and *plans* (AV, RV,
thoughts) will be no less our own for being His: only less burden-
some (*commit* is lit. 'roll', as in Ps. 37:5), and better made.

4. 'Some to honour, some to dishonour'. The AV (*all
things for himself*) is misleading; the phrase is lit. 'everything for
its answer', which may mean either '. . . for its purpose' or
'. . . . for its counterpart'. The final word, *evil, i.e. trouble* (RSV),
may likewise mean either what the wicked suffer or what they
inflict: *cf.* Job 38:23; Isaiah 54:16.

The general meaning is that there are ultimately no loose
ends in God's world: everything will be put to some use and
matched with its proper fate. It does not mean that God is the
author of evil: James 1:13,17.

5. An attitude God hates. The proud man is placed in the
very worst company in Proverbs, heading the 'seven abominations' in 6:17, and assured of judgment, in company with the
adulterer (6:29), the perjuror (19:5), and similar scarlet sinners
whom he doubtless thanks God he does not resemble. See also on
verses 18, 19.

hand . . . in hand (AV, RV): see on 11:21.

6. Genuine religion. The second line indicates that the
mercy (hesed) and truth (better, *loyalty and faithfulness*, RSV) are
man's here, not God's. *Cf.* 20:28. *Purged* (AV, RV) = *atoned for*
(RSV). This is not a denial of grace, but a characteristic demand
for 'fruits that befit repentance'.

7. 'If God be for us . . .'. Other scriptures (*e.g.* Jn. 15:18 ff.) show that this is not a flat statement of law, but an encouragement to fearlessness. 'Consult God's wishes, not man's; He can handle the people you fear!' *Cf.* 29:25.

8. Honesty at all costs. An instructive companion to 15:16, in that it states in absolute moral terms what the latter puts in terms of well-being. See subject-study: God and Man, p. 32.

9. The rightness of God's leading. This companion to verse 1 makes its particular point by the word *directeth*, the Heb. (*cf.* 'established', 12) implying that God has not merely the last word but the soundest. See on 20:24; *cf.* the confession of Jeremiah 10:23, and the prayer of Psalm 119:133.

16:10-15. The burden of power

10. 'Unto whom much is given'. *A divine sentence* (AV, RV) is lit. 'divination', an expression for the finality with which this man speaks. The proverb is a reminder to the king of what is therefore demanded of him (RV: *his mouth shall not transgress . . .*). The Old Testament lends no support to the idea that the king can do no wrong; rather, he is a man under authority: Deuteronomy 17:18-20.

11. God and trade. Some weights and measures were standardized by royal authority (*cf.* 2 Sa. 14:26), and were so inscribed. Here their authorization is taken a step further back. The humblest device to promote fair dealing is God's, like the humblest servant of orderly government (Rom. 13:6). Even the juxtaposition of shopping and salvation in Leviticus 19:36 is scarcely as bold as this. For the negative aspect, see 11:1; 20:10, 23.

12, 13. The king's best interests. These two proverbs build on the assumption that the king is in his right mind – neither deaf to conscience (12b) nor blind to truth (13b). Since most people wield authority in some direction, and are tempted to exchange the proper objects of abomination and delight, the proverb is of more than academic interest.

12b reappears in 25:5; see 25:1-7; 14:34.

14, 15. The king's power. This pair of sayings may be

applied, like 12, 13, to other people than kings. Most of us possess power, as here, to bring misery or happiness to certain people, almost at will, and may play the appalling role of petty tyrant. On the subordinate's part, see on 19:12; 20:2; 25:15.

16:16. Better than gold
See on 8:10,11,19.

16:17. Straight and sure
It is possible to take *evil* to mean 'misfortune', and *soul* (AV, RV) merely *life* (RSV) – in which case the point of the proverb will be that of 15:19, that integrity smooths one's path. But the phrase *depart from evil* (AV, RV) is found also in verse 6, where the context proves it to be moral evil. Our proverb therefore means that the highway consists in shunning what is wrong; and by keeping on this straight course one is guarding one's whole being. *Cf.* 2:10 ff.; 11:3.

16:18, 19. Pride or humility
The special evil of pride is that it opposes the first principle of wisdom (the fear of the Lord) and the two great commandments. The proud man is therefore at odds with himself (8:36), his neighbour (13:10) and the Lord (16:5). *Destruction* may appropriately come from any quarter. See also 18:12.

16:20. Truth and trust
The AV (*he that handleth a matter wisely*), praising both efficiency and faith, is a possible translation. But RV and most moderns rightly find a closer parallelism by taking the Heb. *dābār* (AV: *matter*) in its primary sense of *word* (*he that giveth heed unto the word . . .*). With the brevity of poetry the definite article is omitted before 'word', as in 13:13, where clearly the divine word is meant.

16:21. The charm of wisdom (i)
Learning (AV, RV), here and in 23, should be translated *persuasiveness* (RSV),'as in 7:21 (AV: 'fair speech'); see subject-study:

Wisdom, 1 (5), p. 37. This proverb, and more plainly verse 23, speaks of the impression which true wisdom cannot fail to make. The wise man (not necessarily the clever one) will get known (a) for his discerning eye (AV: *prudent*) and (b) for his telling speech (21b,23). Those who lack judgment or who talk above their hearers' heads need not pine for recognition; only for wisdom.

16:22. You must live with yourself
See subject-study: Life and Death, p. 54.

Understanding (AV, RV) is *śekel*: 'good sense' (see subject-study: Wisdom, 1 (3), p. 36); *instruction* (AV) should be *chastisement* (RSV): *i.e.* the fool makes a rod for his back.

16:23. The charm of wisdom (ii)
See comment on verse 21.

16:24. Sweetening is not superfluous
This balances 21 and 23 (see note), which otherwise might look too calculating. To say nice things when we can is a simple benefit we may bring a person, in mind and thence in body. *Cf.* 12:25, and subject-study: Words, 1 (1), p. 46.

16:25. The deceptive road
This repeats, and so underlines, 14:12. *Cf.* 16:9.

16:26. Incentive to hard work
AV misses the point, which RSV makes well: *A worker's appetite works for him; his mouth urges him on.* The work in question is toil; hence Knox: 'No better friend drudgery has than appetite; hunger drives a man to his task.' This is welcome realism (*cf.* 2 Thes. 3:10–12), though it is not the last word on incentives: *cf.* Ephesians 4:28; 6:7.

16: 27–30. Mischief-makers
Plots, invective (27), or a mere whisper (28); toughness (29), or subtlety (30) – here are ways enough of spreading damage. See subject-study: Words, 1 (2), p. 47.

27. *Diggeth up* (AV): rather, *diggeth*: a stock word for plotting, from digging a pit (*cf.* 26:27, *etc.*).

28. *Soweth* (AV): rather, *spreads* (RSV). It is, appropriately, the word used of the release of flaming foxes in the Philistines' corn, Judges 15:5. *Cf.* Proverbs 17:9.

30. *Shutteth . . . moving* (AV): RSV has *winks . . . compresses*, indicating, as in 6:13, the wealth of meaning, and of mischief, that can be disseminated without a word spoken.

16:31. Beauty of age
The AV's *if* reads too much into the Heb. Without it, the meaning is that this *crown* is the natural reward (but not, of course, the monopoly – see, *e.g.*, Jb. 21:7) of right living; *cf.* 3:1, 2. *Glory* should be rendered 'beauty'; see further 20:29, and note.

16:32. Self-control
Cf. 14:17,29; 25:28; 29:11. James 1:19,20 adds a still stronger argument.

16:33. God, not chance, decides
The Old Testament use of the word *lot* shows that this proverb (and 18:18) is not about God's control of all random occurrences, but about His settling of matters properly referred to Him. Land was 'allotted' (Jos. 14:1,2), likewise temple service (1 Ch. 25:8); probably the Urim and Thummim were lots. But God's last use of this method was, significantly, the last event before Pentecost (Acts 1:26); thereafter He has no longer guided His church as a 'servant' who 'knoweth not what his lord doeth': *cf.* Acts 13:2; 15:25,28.

17:1. Blessed tranquillity
Cf. 15:17. The last phrase here, lit. 'strife-offerings', is a sharp parody. A family feast consisted usually of a peace-offering (Dt. 12:11,12,21; 1 Sa. 20:6), but human frailty might allow it as little peace as Elkanah's (1 Sa. 1:3–7), and as little religious content as a drinking-party (Pr. 7:13,14).

17:2. Ability outruns privilege

Privilege, as an obstacle or a support, looms larger in most people's minds than in God's, in things both spiritual (Am. 9:7; Mt. 8:11,12) and temporal. Solomon's proverb was to be strikingly borne out in the careers of his servant and his son (1 Ki. 11:28 ff.).

17:3. The crucible

Cf. 27:21. The second line by itself would make God only an examiner; but the first line implies that His trials are constructive: not for finding a person out but for sorting him out. When things reveal their relative worths under 'fiery trial', it is our part (since we are not inert metal) to pick out, with Him, 'the precious from the worthless' (see Je. 15:19), for the benefit is not automatic (Je. 6:29,30).

17:4. Guilty listener

Evil words die without a welcome; and the welcome gives us away (see subject-study: Words, II (3), p. 47). Another side of the listener's role appears in verse 10.

17:5. Heartlessness

To grow into this monster one has only to stay long enough a spoilt child. For God's interest in this matter, see on 14:31 and 16:5.

17:6. Harmony of age and youth

Cf. 16:31. These fine family fruits need cultivating and protecting. A neglected crop, riddled with mutual antipathy, is seen in Isaiah 3:5; Micah 7:6; 2 Timothy 3:2–4.

17:7. Be what you profess

Excellent (AV, RV) or *fine* (RSV): the word suggests excess, hence talking 'big'. (LXX has 'reliable', reading the root *yšr* for *ytr*.)

Fool is *nāḇāl* (as in 17:21b; 30:22): the overbearing, crudely godless man as in Psalm 14:1 or 1 Samuel 25:25. The contrast between him and the *prince* (*nāḏîḇ*) or, better, 'nobleman', is clarified in Isaiah 32:5-8, where both words occur, and nobility is made a title to be lived up to.

17:8. Bribery

Gift (AV, RV) is here *bribe* (RSV; *šoḥad*, never used of a disinterested gift).

Precious stone (AV, RV) is lit. 'stone of favour'; hence RSV hazards *magic stone*, as procuring favour. The saying's general sense is clear: it describes the briber's confidence in the versatile usefulness of his tool. 'Money talks.' But God's view is given in verses 15 and 23.

17:9. Peacemaker, troublemaker

The first line inverts 10:12b (where see note) and completes the circle, for love seeks love, not ascendancy.

For the second line, *cf.* 16:28b. *Repeateth* may indicate either tale-telling or (as RV) harping on a matter. *Chief friends* (RV) is a single word, denoting a bosom companion.[1] For other occurrences see note on 2:17.

17:10. The will to improve

See subject-study: The Fool, II (1), p. 40.

Entereth more (AV): 'sinks deeper' (Moffatt).

Cf. Ahikar, xv (*DOTT*, p. 272): 'Smite a man with a wise word that it may be in his heart like a fever in summer; . . . smite a fool with many rods, he will not perceive it.'

17:11. Playing with fire

Subject and object should be reversed here, as the Heb. suggests. So Moffatt, succinctly: 'Rebels are out for mischief.' That is to say, since rebellion scorns moderation, the rebel need expect none, for what we seek, we find. See also verse 13.

17:12. Fool on the prowl

See subject-study: The Fool, II (1), p. 40.

---

[1] Or possibly, as a collective term, 'a fellowship'; see J. Gray, *The Legacy of Canaan* (1957), p. 31.

17:13. Home to roost
This proverb was very near the bone: both parents of Solomon had so repaid the devoted Uriah, and had duly received the sentence of line 2 : see 2 Samuel 12:10 ff. The happier corollary of this principle is found in 1 Peter 3:9. See also note on 20:22.

17:14. Anger's havoc
Before it be meddled with (AV): rather, *. . . breaks out* (RSV). The verb recurs only in 18:1; 20:3. Opening such a sluice lets loose more than one can predict, control or retrieve.

17:15. Injustice
Moffatt: 'The Eternal loathes the pair of them.' *Cf.* the Law and the Prophets (Ex. 23:7; Is. 5:23). It is the strong Old Testament background to the New Testament's exultant news of Romans 4:5 and 3:26 (AV): '. . . that he might be just, and the justifier . . .'

17:16. Wisdom not for sale
See subject-study: The Fool, II (1), p. 40.
   Heart can mean 'will' (*cf.* AV) or *mind* (RSV, see also RV); probably both here. Moffatt neatly retains the *double-entendre* with 'when he has no mind to learn'.

17:17. Friend in need
See subject-studies: The Friend, I (b), p. 45, and The Family, III, p. 52.
   RVmg ('and is born as a brother') is possible but a little far-fetched. The meaning is rather that in trouble you see what family ties are for, and you also see who are your friends. But the next verse shows that a friend may be unfairly imposed upon.

17:18. Unlimited liability
This is no contradiction of 17. It deprecates, not help for a friend in need, but a blind guarantee which may lead the recipient to rashness, and both to ruin. See further on 6:1–5.

17:19. Asking for trouble

The Heb. order slightly favours RSV, RVmg, *i.e.*, freely, 'Love sin, love strife', which accords with line 2 in saying that arrogance, Godward and manward, must be paid for. *Cf.* Shebna's pretentiousness: Isaiah 22:16ff.

17:20. Too clever

11:20 warns of God's abhorrence; the present proverb (like verse 19), of temporal trouble. Contrast 8:8. On *froward* (AV, RV), see on 2:14,15.

17:21. Disappointing son

Cf. verse 25, and 10:1; 15:20; see also subject-study: The Fool, II(1), p. 40. The second fool is a *nāḇāl*: see on verse 7.

For a wider application, see Hebrews 13:7; 3 John 4.

17:22. The best medicine

Cf. 12:25; 15:13,15; 18:14.

17:23. The bribe

See on verse 8.

17:24. One thing is needful

Wisdom is 'straight in front of' the discerning man, in two senses: (a) he *sets his face toward* it (RSV), unlike the fool; and (b) he cannot miss it. Both senses are in James 1:5–8. *Cf.* subject-study: The Fool, II (1), p. 40.

17:25. Exasperating son

Grief is a sharper word than the 'sorrow' of verse 21 (AV, RV); *cf.* 'provoking', Deuteronomy 32:19; 1 Kings 15:30, *etc.*

17:26. Innocent blood

The *also* (AV, RV) with which this proverb properly begins may indicate that it was once paired with another, such as 18:5, which it resembles and goes beyond. In 18:5 the man in the right loses his lawsuit; here, he is fined or flogged.

But 'also' can equally mean 'even' (as in 28): 'Even to fine an innocent man is bad; [much more,] to flog noble men for their uprightness'; a powerful comparison, and an apt comment on political or religious persecution. The only question is whether poetic terseness would have gone so far as to omit the words in brackets.

On *princes* (AV), see on verse 7.

17:27, 28. Think before you speak
The AV spoils the second line of 27 by accepting an unnecessary Massoretic alteration. Read with RV: *he that is of a cool spirit is a man of understanding. Cf.* note on 14:17, and subject-study: Words, III, p. 48.

The dry advice of 28 is not purely ironical: the fool who takes it is no longer a complete fool. *Cf.* 18:2; Ecclesiastes 10:12–14.

18:1. Doggedly out of step
RV, by supplying two words, makes sense of the text as a proverb on boorish irresponsibility: *He that separateth himself seeketh (his own) desire, and rageth against all sound wisdom.* But LXX has '. . . seeketh pretexts', reading a Heb. text different from ours by one consonant. Since the same Heb. phrase for 'seek an occasion' appears in Judges 14:4, RSV seems justified in adopting this. Knox puts it: 'None so quick to find pretexts, as he that would break with a friend . . .'

18:2. Closed mind, open mouth
RSV and Moffatt, between them, display the double edge of the second line. RSV: *but only in expressing his opinion*; Moffatt: 'but only in displaying what he is'. The verb, found elsewhere in this form only in Genesis 9:21, hints that decency itself is affronted.

18:3. Sin's travelling companions
Wickedness (RSV) seems a preferable reading of the Heb. consonants to *the wicked* (AV, RV). The three terms for shame give triple emphasis to this corollary of sin (the antithesis of the glory which is the corollary of holiness: Is. 6:3; Rom. 8:30); and the

Bible elsewhere shows it to be one of sin's first (Gn. 3:7) and final (Dn. 12:2) fruits.

18:4. Wisdom's sparkling flow
Comparison with 20:5 suggests that the *deep waters* stand for concealment,

> 'For words, like Nature, half reveal
> And half conceal the Soul within.'[1]

If this is so, the proverb is contrasting our human reluctance, or inability, to give ourselves away, with the refreshing candour and clarity of the true wisdom.

18:5. Favouritism
See on 28:21; 17:26.

18:6, 7. Talking oneself into trouble
Enter (6, AV, RV): the Heb. can be read as a causative, *i.e.* 'bring (him)'; so LXX. Moffatt puts it well: 'A fool's talk gets him into trouble' (*i.e.* strife).

Cf. subject-study: The Fool, II (1), p. 40.

18:8. Titbits of gossip
Delicious morsels (RSV) is a more likely translation than AV's *wounds*; modern scholars agree in deriving it from a verb 'to swallow greedily'. See subject-study: Words, I (1), p. 46.

The proverb is exactly repeated in 26:22.

18:9. Slacker and wrecker
Waster (AV) means one who lays waste, not who wastes time. 'The sage teaches that he who leaves a work undone is next of kin to him who destroys it' (Oesterley). *Cf.* 28:24. See subject-study: The Sluggard, I, pp. 42f.

18:10, 11. Strong tower; castle in the air
The world thinks that the unseen is the unreal. But it is not the

1 Tennyson, *In Memoriam*, v.

man of God (10) but the man of property, who must draw on *his imagination* (11c, AV, RV, RSVmg) to feel secure.

In 10b, *safe* implies being 'safely above' the danger; a similar expression is used in 29:25.

18:12. Pride and humility
Cf. 15:33; see note on 16:18,19.

18:13. Jumping to conclusions
A special snare of the self-important. Verse 2 (see note) gives a pungent comment, and verse 17 a further consideration.

18:14. The mainspring
Short of outward resources, life is hard; short of inward, it is insupportable. It has been well said, accordingly, that in praying for one another we should observe the sequence found in 1 Thessalonians 5:23.

Cf. 12:25; 15:13.

18:15. A mind with an appetite
The repetition, *knowledge* . . . *knowledge* is for emphasis, and the emphasis is on no platitude, but on the paradox that those who know most know best how little they know. See 1 Corinthians 8:2; Philippians 3:10ff.

Cf. 15:14.

18:16. Paving the way
Gift (*mattān*) is a more neutral word than that of 17:8,23 (*šōḥaḏ*). Its danger is implied in 21:14 (see note), and pointed out in 15:27 (see note), but it can also be an innocent courtesy or eirenicon, like the present (*minḥah*) sent to the captain in 1 Samuel 17:18, or to Esau or Joseph (Gn. 32:20; 43:11).

18:17. Hear both sides
RSV is clearer than the older versions: *He who states his case first seems right, until the other comes and examines him.* It is the third warning in this chapter against forming hasty opinions (see 2 and 13).

18:18. In His will is our peace
The Christian equivalent of the implied advice of this proverb
is to seek God's leading, when interests or opinions clash, and to
accept it with a good grace. On drawing lots, see note on 16:33.

18:19. Stubborn defences
The italics in AV, RV, show how laconic is the original. RSV follows
LXX in part, but it presupposes changes in two of the four Heb.
words of the first line. From line 2 it seems that AV, RV are on the
right path, and the proverb so understood is a forceful warning
of the strength of the invisible walls of estrangement, so easy to
erect, so hard to demolish.

18:20, 21. Your words will catch up with you
The second of this pair of proverbs, with its warning to the
talkative, throws a sobering light on the first. Both of them urge
caution, for *satisfied* (20) can mean 'sated': the meaning, good
or bad, will depend on the care taken. Moffatt paraphrases 20
well, but one-sidedly: 'A man must answer for his utterances,
and take the consequences of his words.' Oesterley quotes the
witty saying of Ahikar: 'My son, sweeten thy tongue, and make
savoury the opening of thy mouth; for the tail of a dog gives
him bread, and his mouth gets him blows.'

18:22. A fine wife
The wording, especially in the Heb., strikingly resembles that
of 8:35, and so suggests that after wisdom itself, the best of God's
blessings is a good wife. 31:10 makes a similar comparison,
putting her price, like wisdom's (8:11), above rubies. It is
implicit here, and explicit in, *e.g.*, 19:13,14, that not any and
every wife is in mind: see, by contrast, 14:1; 21:9! *A good thing*
(lit. 'good'): better, 'a boon'.

18:23. Harsh realities
Such detached reporting, with its pointed lack of comment,
faces the reader with the ugliness of the world he lives in (*cf.* the

toadying and the heartlessness in 19:4,6,7; contrast the ways of God), and reminds him to take its pains and prizes calmly (*cf.* Jas. 1:9,10; 5:6, 7). For an explicit evaluation, see 19:1.

18:24. A friend worth the name
The first line reads lit. 'A man of friends [is] to be shattered'. The verb is a play on the Heb. for 'to make friends' (found in 22:24); but it is not the same word, as AV (*must shew himself friendly*) and RSV would prefer. (RSV reads: *There are friends who pretend to be friends.*) The RV gives the most probable sense of the Heb. text: *He that maketh many friends (doeth it) to his own destruction.* But the Heb. is very cryptic, and there is a case for reading the opening word (*cf.* RSV) not as 'a-man-of', but as 'there-are' (a very small consonantal difference):[1] *i.e.*, 'There are friends to (one's) undoing'. King Zedekiah was warned of this (Je. 38:22), but in vain.

The second line emphasizes the contrast by using a more positive word for friend: see subject-study: The Friend, 1 (b), p. 45.

19:1. 'How much is he worth?'
By distinguishing tacitly between *better* and 'better-off', and between 'wise' and 'clever' (for *perverse* here means twisty), this couplet sharply exposes the false values behind the behaviour reported in verses 6 and 7 (see also notes on 18:23; 19:22).

The first line recurs at 28:6, where it is matched by a closer-fitting but less scathing second, which the Syr. and Targ. (followed by Moffatt) substitute here needlessly for the present one.

19:2. Getting nowhere, fast
The *also* (omitted in RSV) is important, as a link with verse 1,

---

[1] G. R. Driver (*Biblica*, 1951, pp. 183f.) keeps the text intact by taking the debated verb to be from *rûa'*, 'to shout', weakened to 'to chatter'. That is, 'A man of (many) friends (is a friend only) for chattering together' – good company, but no stand-by. But this weakened sense, in spite of a Syriac parallel, remains a conjecture.

confronting the 'better' of that proverb with the *not good* of this. *Knowledge* (*i.e.* of God, as Proverbs always teaches) is the real wealth; notice how negative is the achievement of the man who wants tangible and quick rewards (*sinneth*, AV, RV = *misses his way*, RSV; *cf.* Jdg. 20:16).

19:3. Always God's fault
The modern versions bring out the point implied by the Heb.'s emphatic *against the Lord*: *i.e.* God gets blamed for what we bring on ourselves.

19:4. Fair-weather friends
See also 6, 7, and notes on 18:23,24.

19:5. Perjury
See on 14:25. This is a statement made in faith, for perjurers may escape human justice. Even the stern law of Deuteronomy 19:18–21 availed nothing for Naboth – or for Jesus. The matter is grave enough for virtual repetition in verse 9.

19:6, 7. Fair-weather friends
See verse 4, and notes on 18:23,24. With 6a, *cf.* 29:26.

19:8. Sense pays its way
Wisdom here is 'sense', the same word (lit. 'heart') as in Hosea 7:11 and Proverbs 15:32b. The present saying makes a good climax to the latter. It is paralleled, at a deeper level, in 8:35,36.

19:9. Perjury
See verse 5.

19:10. Pearls and swine
Delight (AV) here means *luxury* (RSV). While God loves to surprise the undeserving with grace, it is to ennoble them; He has no pleasure in a misfit. Other proverbs on jarring absurdities are 11:22; 17:7; 26:1; 30:21–23.

19:11. Magnanimity

Good sense (RSV) and *glory* point to the practical and the moral worth of this quality; both of them amply demonstrated by the early history of David. The word for *glory* is sometimes translated 'beauty' (*e.g.* Ex. 28:2): it suggests adornment, and so brings out here the glowing colours of a virtue which in practice may look drably unassertive. God Himself declares His 'almighty power most chiefly in showing mercy and pity' (the Collect for the Eleventh Sunday after Trinity).

19:12. The lion and the dew

See notes on 16:14,15; 20:2. Subordinates may learn tact here, and superiors pleasantness. Perhaps the position of this proverb next to verse 11 emphasizes for the benefit of the powerful the quiet fruitfulness of the latter quality. *Cf.* David's ideal of a ruler, 2 Samuel 23:3,4; and God's pledge to Israel, Hosea 14:5.

19:13, 14. Hell or heaven at home

13. *Contentions* (AV, RV): Moffatt has, excellently, 'nagging'. On the simile of dripping water (treated more fully in 27:15,16) Delitzsch passes on an Arab proverb told him by Wetzstein, which runs (in Toy's more compact summary): 'Three things make a house intolerable: *tak* (the leaking through of rain), *nak* (a wife's nagging) and *bak* (bugs).'

14. *From the Lord* is emphatic, and rightly preceded in RV, RSV, by *but*. It implies that this gift is beyond both comparison and contriving. *Cf.* 18:22 and, for an expansion of *prudent*, 31:10–31.

19:15. The creeping spread of sloth

Here is its inward and outward progress, for it is not static like its victims. See subject-study: The Sluggard, II (2), p. 43.

19:16. The soul that sinneth ...

See on 13:13, and subject-study: Life and Death, p. 56. The sense of *despiseth* is well given in RV as *is careless of*. The Heb.

consonantal text has the stronger expression 'shall be put to death' for *shall die*, a striking reminder of the seriousness of sins of omission, and of a Judge (not merely a natural process) to be reckoned with.

19:17. 'Ye did it unto me'

That which he hath given (AV) should be *his deed* (RSV). It promises faithful recompense, not necessarily one's money back!

19:18. Deadly leniency

The second line should be rendered, as in RV, RSV, *set not thy heart* (*cf.* Ho. 4:8; Ezk. 24:25) *on his destruction*. To withhold discipline is neither a compliment nor a kindness; and the opportunity passes: *cf.* 1 Kings 1:5,6. See subject-study: The Family, II, p. 51.

19:19. His own worst enemy

The Heb. text is cryptic and perhaps damaged (*great* is a marginal correction, in the Heb., of an obscure word), but RV, RSV, agree with AV's interpretation: *i.e.* an ungovernable temper will repeatedly land its owner in fresh trouble.

19:20. Wisdom a long-term investment

On the characteristic forward look, see note on 5:4. See also article: Wisdom, II, pp. 37f.

19:21. Man proposes, God disposes

For varied aspects of this theme, see 16:1, 9, and notes.

19:22. A man's true worth

A clue to *the desire of* (AV, RV) may be in Genesis 49:26, where the same expression (mistranslated in AV, RV as 'utmost bound') means 'desirable things' (*cf.* the parallel 'precious things' in Dt. 33:15). This supports RSV's rendering here: *What is desired in a man is loyalty*, which prepares well for the second line. *Cf.* verse 1. This *loyalty* (AV: *kindness*) is the *ḥeseḏ*, 'loyal love' which is the bond between those who are truly in covenant.

RV, rather less probably, makes *desire* signify 'good intention', by supplying the idea of measuring a good deed's value.

19:23. Godliness satisfies

Cf. 11:19, and subject-study: Life and Death, p. 54.

The Heb. text of the second line is extremely abrupt, and perhaps damaged.

19:24. The sluggard's inertia

Bosom (AV) should be *dish* (RV, RSV); the same word in 2 Kings 21:13 leaves no doubt of its meaning. The scene is thus a meal, and the example comically extreme. See subject-study: The Sluggard, 1 (2), p. 42. 26:15 repeats this almost exactly.

19:25. The language a fool understands

Here are three varieties of mind: closed (the *scorner*, AV, RV; *cf.* verse 29; 9:7,8), empty (the *simple* – he must be startled into attention), and open (the discerning – he accepts even a painful truth).

Cf. 21:11, and subject-study: The Fool, 1, 111, pp. 39, 42.

19:26. Unnatural son

The second line is not the anticlimax which at first glance it may appear to be, for the ruin (*wasteth*, AV) and eviction are overshadowed by the special bitterness of receiving them from a son. *Cf.* the poignant emphasis in Isaiah 1:2: 'Sons have I nourished . . .'. See subject-study: The Family, 11, p. 51.

19:27. Trifling with truth

The AV contains two improbabilities: (a) that *instruction*, unqualified, should have a bad sense in Proverbs; (b) that *to err* should mean 'to cause to err' (for which Heb. has an appropriate expression). RV, RSV seem justified in taking it as an outcry against trifling (RV: *Cease . . . to hear instruction (only) to err from . . . knowledge*). *Cf.* 17:16; 2 Peter 2:21.

19:28. Deliberate distortion

Ungodly (AV) is lit. 'of Belial', on which see note on 6:12, and *cf.* 1 Kings 21:10. The second line delves beneath the cynicism to the craving for what is tainted. One may see here, far advanced, the spiritual morbidity which betrays its presence whenever one enjoys giving a malicious twist to a story.

19:29. When warnings fail
Cf. verse 25, and note; also 26:3.

20:1. 'Under the influence . . .'
The opposite of the humble alertness and diligence of the disciple of wisdom (*e.g.* 19:20) is the mood of dogmatism (*mocker* is the same word as 'scorner' or 'scoffer' in the previous verse) and aggressiveness (*raging*, AV; *a brawler*, RV, RSV) induced by strong drink (which is given here, poetically, a personality dominating the drinker).

Is deceived (AV), or, *is not wise* (RV, RSV): this word can also mean 'lurches' (*cf.* Is. 28:7), a *double-entendre*!

23:29–35 enlarges on this theme vividly.

20:2. Tactlessness
Cf. 19:12; but here the warning is explicit. AV's *fear of* means 'fear inspired by'. *Sinneth . . . soul* (AV), not in the theological sense, but (as RSV) meaning *forfeits his life*.

20:3. 'Not easily provoked'
Cease (AV): rather, *keep aloof* (RV, RSV). *Meddling* (AV): rather, *quarrelling* (RV, RSV), as (only) in 17:14; 18:1.

To spring to the defence of one's honour is to do it a disservice; *cf.* Jephthah, in contrast with Gideon: Judges 12:1–6; 8:1–3.

20:4. The sluggard's softness
By reason of (lit. 'from', used causally) *the cold*: AV is supported by RV and Vulg.; but most commentators, and RSV, prefer *in* (lit. 'from', used temporally) *the autumn*, which makes it simple procrastination. But 'autumn' can mean 'cold season' (Je. 36:22; Gn. 8:22), and it would seem likely that the discomfort of it is the excuse the sluggard wants.

Beg (AV, RV): possibly from his fields rather than his neigh-bours; hence RSV's *seek*.

See subject-study: The Sluggard, 1, p. 42.

20:5. Fathoming one's fellow men

It is foreign to the thought of Proverbs to gather from this that every man has an inner reservoir of wisdom, and the wise man is simply the man who can draw upon it (see, against the idea, 14:12; 16:22). Rather, the proverb concerns that insight into human nature which Proverbs aims to impart, whereby a discerning person can bring to light the deepest intentions (rather than AV, RV's *counsel*) of another. *Cf.* the note on verse 8.

The simile of *deep water* is found also in 18:4, where see note.

20:6. Yours faithfully

The contrast is between profession and reality, not between goodness (*ḥeseḏ*) and faithfulness, both of which contain the idea of steadfastness (the former with overtones of covenant and pledge: see on 19:22). See subject-study: The Friend, 1 (b), p. 45.

20:7. A father's best legacy

This is (as in RV, RSV) one statement, not two. Lit. 'A righteous man walking in his integrity – happy are . . .' It answers the temptation to 'get on' at all costs 'for the children's sake'.

20:8. An eye for character

Scattereth means primarily *winnoweth* (RVmg, RSV); and in verse 26 the threshing-wheel confirms this translation. The practised eye of a true ruler sifts the chaff from the wheat; still surer is the Spirit of the Lord: Isaiah 11:3; 1 Corinthians 2:15.

20:9. Where self-help fails

Cf. verse 12, and note; also subject-study: God and Man, pp. 32f.

20:10. Short weight

Cf. verse 23, and note on 11:1.

20:11. A child's character

An important verse, revealing God's interest in children as such; not only as adults in the making. In the Heb., the word *even* is followed by *by his doings* (AV, RV), and evidently qualifies the sentence as a whole, not just the word *child*. Etymologically, a case can be made for the rendering: 'Even in his play, a child makes himself known' (Ewald's suggestion; *cf.* Knox). This is attractive, because it gives point to the word-order, and a thought-provoking meaning; but the crucial noun does not appear to have this sense elsewhere.

20:12. By grace alone

Hearing is the Heb. term for 'obedient' (so translated in 25:12; *cf.* 15:31; 1 Sa. 15:22). It can also, like 'seeing', express understanding: *cf.* Isaiah 6:9,10. The proverb makes a constructive companion to verse 9, pointing with it towards Ephesians 2:8-10.

20:13. Early to rise

See subject-study: The Sluggard, pp. 42f.

20:14. The bargain-driver

Naught (AV, RV) is lit. *bad* (RSV). Knox: 'A poor thing, says the buyer, a poor thing! Then off he goes, and boasts of it.' We may find here a sketch; also a businessman's warning to the inexperienced; perhaps, too, a parable, for there are also immaterial assets which we can be talked into selling lightly (Heb. 12:16).

20:15. Precious jewel

See 3:14,15, and note on 8:10,11; but here the contrast is between kinds of adornment, not of wealth. To be justly admired, study to catch the ear, not the eye; and offer it things of more than scarcity-value.

20:16. Hostage to fortune

A strange woman (AV, line 2): so reads the twin proverb, 27:13;

138

but the Heb. consonants in our verse read 'strangers' (masc. plural); *cf.* RV, RSV. *Take his garment* means: 'Don't lend to him without security (Ex. 22:26); he is a bad risk!' See note on 6:1–5.

20:17. Sin's aftertaste
Cf. the equally striking sequel to 9:17; also note on 5:4.

20:18. Be open to advice
See note on 11:14.

20:19. Beware of a gossip
One *that flattereth*: rather, 'a babbler'; the verb is associated with *peṭi*, simpleton, fool. The point of the first line is that it may be *your* secrets next. See also on 11:13.

20:20. Unfilial behaviour
See subject-study: The Family, II, p. 51. The modern habit is to evaluate the person rather than the office (*e.g.* to be respectful to one's master or faithful to one's partner if they *evoke* such a response, not because it is *owed* to them in their position). The Old Testament law instilled the opposite attitude from childhood, and the New Testament supports it (*e.g.* Eph. 6:1–9; 1 Pet. 2:13–18). See also 30:11,17.

20:21. The final audit
A companion to 13:11. There, the emphasis is on the inherent instability of easy money; here, on the forfeiting of God's blessing by (implied) dishonesty. See also the next verse, and 21:5, 6; 28:20, 22.

20:22. Sweeter than vengeance
The certainty that God is Saviour (and, verse 21, Judge) is the answer to selfish haste. An ascending scale can be constructed, from 17:13 through 20:22 and 24:29 to 25:21.

20:23. Fraud
Cf. verse 10, and see note on 11:1.

20:24. Planned route

The emphases fall on *the Lord* and *man*. The saying is relevant both to the Lord's prescribed part for us to play (Ps. 37:23; our improvising cannot compare with His composing) and to His overruling of us (we cannot see what order He will bring from our confusion: *cf.* Gn. 50:20; 1 Ki. 12:15). See further on 16:9.

20:25. Count the cost

The style is cryptic, and certain words are of doubtful meaning; but the key words are *holy* and *vows*. Moffatt is, with RSV, probably near the mark: ' 'Tis perilous to say rashly "This is sacred!" and then reconsider your vow.' (*Say rashly* (RSV; *cf.* RV) fits Jb. 6:3, better than AV's *devoureth*.) To pronounce a thing sacred is to dedicate it. Here, then, is an impulsive man, pledging more than he seriously intends. *Cf.* Ecclesiastes 5:5: 'Better . . . not vow, than . . . vow and not pay.'

20:26. Strong government

See note on verse 8. There, the emphasis is on discrimination; here, on action. The counterpoise to this aspect of authority comes in verse 28.

20:27. Conscience

The figure is of a lamp carried from room to room, and flashed into the darkest corners. *Cf.* verse 30, and note. *Spirit*, here, is lit. 'breath': *cf.* Genesis 2:7.

20:28. Severity is not enough

For *mercy* (AV, RV), substitute 'love' (*ḥeseḏ*, the pledged love of those who are in covenant; *cf.* note on 19:22). Line 2 repeats the vital word ('And he upholds his throne by love'). The principle of the proverb, which is the complement of verse 26, applies with equal force to lesser forms of authority.

20:29. Beauty of youth and age

A proverb to lift the reader above the unfruitful attitudes of envy, impatience and contempt which the old and the young may adopt towards each other. Each age has its appointed excellence, to be respected and enjoyed in its time. *Cf.* 16:31.

20:30. Corporal punishment

AV's *blueness* is from Vulg., and obscures the Heb.'s 'strokes of bruising (or, cutting)', *i.e.* 'a severe beating'. The final phrase, echoing verse 27 (see note), shows that where conscience is sluggish it may need such a spur.

The paradox of Isaiah 53:5 stands out sharply against this background: that with *His* stripes *we* are healed.

21:1. King of kings

Rivers (AV) should be *watercourses* (RV), *i.e.* irrigation canals, under the farmer's control: *cf.* Deuteronomy 11:10. This is a saying about providence, not regeneration. Tiglath-pileser (Is. 10:6,7), Cyrus (Is. 41:2–4) and Artaxerxes (Ezr. 7:21) are all examples of autocrats who, in pursuing their chosen courses, flooded or fertilized God's field as He chose. The principle is still in force.

21:2. Weighed in the balances

Pondereth (AV) is the same word as 'weigheth' in 16:2, which this saying virtually repeats. The contrast between our guessing and God's knowing is important enough for re-emphasis.

21:3. God cannot be bought

See on 15:8, and subject-study: God and Man, pp. 31ff.

21:4. Lofty unconcern

Plowing (AV) should almost certainly be *lamp* (AVmg, RV, RSV). Comparison with 13:9 (see note) and with 2 Samuel 21:17; 22:29; 1 Kings 11:36, suggests that the lamp stands for life and hope. For the godly, these are God-given; for the wicked, man-made. If we take 'the lamp' as summing up the first line (as RV), *i.e.* as 'their arrogant life', then *sin* is a fair epithet for it. If we take it as a third item, the word for sin may be understood in its non-ethical sense of 'error'. So Knox, freely: 'Lordly looks, proud heart; the hopes of the wicked are all at fault.'

21:5. Thoroughness tells

Thoughts (AV, RV) should be *plans* (RSV), as always with this word (*e.g.* 16:3; Je. 29:11). The Heb. for *hasty* (*cf.* 28:20) suggests the thruster rather than the slapdash. On the 'get-rich-quick' theme, see also the next verse, and note on 20:21 (which uses a different word). On *plenteousness* (AV, RV) and *want*, *cf.* 14:23.

21:6. Ill-gotten, ill-fated

This verse is a companion to 5 and 7. The second line is abrupt and spluttering: 'a driven vapour – seekers of death'. There are three main ways of integrating it with the first line: (a) by pronouncing the Heb. for *getting* (line 1) as 'getter' (so LXX), and taking 'seekers' as meaning 'all such are seekers'; (b) by filling out line 2 as in RV; (c) by taking 'seekers' to be a miscopying of a similar word, *snares* (LXX, Vulg., RVmg, RSV).

21:7. Their own executioners

See verses 5,6. *Cf.* Abimelech and the Shechemites, self-destroyed by the power-politics they embraced: Judges 9:23,24.

21:8. Clear conscience, clear path

Guilty (RSV) is Heb. *wāzār*, occurring only here; its meaning is deduced from one of two Arabic roots (RV's *laden with guilt* uses both!). The AV (*wā = and*; *zār = strange*) creates an awkward antithesis.

21:9. The scold

Against AV, RV, the RSV, fortified by the ancient versions, resists the temptation to transpose two Heb. consonants and thereby alter *a house shared* (Heb. text; lit., 'a house of company')[1] to 'a spacious house'. So it preserves the choice between ignominious solitude and intolerable society.

The saying recurs at 25:24. *Cf.* also verse 19; 19:13,14 (and note); 27:15,16.

---

[1] Albright (*WIANE*, p. 12) tries to make this a 'public house', *i.e.*, an ale-house. A better suggestion, by J. J. Finkelstein (*JBL*, 1956, pp. 328ff.), translates the phrase as 'a noisy household', from an Accadian root.

21:10. Bent upon evil

An important truth about depravity: men can sin not merely from weakness but eagerly and ruthlessly. The expression *the soul . . . desireth* is commonly the language of both proper appetite (*e.g.* Dt. 12:20) and ambition (2 Sa. 3:21). In happier contrast see Isaiah 26:9.

21:11. Degrees of teachability

See note on 19:25.

21:12. Justice will be done

Literally this runs: 'A-righteous-one (Heb. *ṣaddîq*) considers the house of a-wicked-one, (and) overthrows wicked-ones into calamity.' This yields sense most easily if we take this Righteous One to be God. Such a use of the bare adjective is not unknown: *cf.* Job 34:17, also a similar use of 'holy' in Isaiah 40:25; Habakkuk 3:3; Job 6:10. Otherwise we must assume the righteous one to mean a righteous ruler, or take liberties with the text.

21:13. His turn will come

Cf. the searching demands of 24:11,12; 25:21. The ultimate comments are the story of Dives and Lazarus (Lk. 16:19–31) and the judgment scene of Matthew 25:31–46.

21:14. Gifts and bribes

Here the neutral term *gift* (*mattān*) is coupled with the bad term *bribe* (RSV; *šōḥaḏ*), a reminder that the boundary between the two is thin at the best of times, and is crossed at this point by the secrecy of the transaction. *Cf.* the warning in 15:27 (see note).

21:15. Justice – friend or foe?

To do judgment (AV, RV) can mean 'the execution of justice' (Toy); hence RSV: *When justice is done, it is a joy to the righteous, but dismay to evildoers.* But the phrase is usually an expression for right conduct (*cf.* 7b), and we may take *dismay* to be the sinner's reaction to the thought of doing right, and *joy* to be the righteous man's actual experience of it (see note on 17). Line 2 is found also at 10:29.

21:16. Moral wanderlust
Every word of the second line is charged with irony. The rebel, who must roam at will, is only hastening to lose his mobility (*shall rest*, RV), his independence (*in the congregation*, AV, RV) and his life (*of the dead*).

21:17. The price of pleasure-seeking
Pleasure is the same word as 'joy' in verse 15, and the two sayings contrast two ways of life. The just man seeks to act fairly, and finds joy as he does so (15); the pleasure-lover strikes out towards joy itself, and finds poverty. Between the two verses comes the grim warning (16) that more than pleasure is at stake. Verses 20, 21, teach a similar lesson, materially and spiritually.

21:18. The unjust for the just
This saying (with 11:8) acts as a pointer to the paradox of the atonement, in that it defines those who might fairly be called the 'expendable' members of society. Isaiah 43:3,4 uses such language for the fall of nations which cleared the path of Cyrus to Babylon and the liberation of Israel; Luke 13:1-5 warns us however against reading all events in such terms. Against this background we can appreciate the reversal of the roles in Mark 10:45; 1 Peter 3:18, *etc.*

21:19. The scold
Cf. verse 9, and note on 19:13.

21:20, 21. Material and spiritual treasure
See note on 17. In verse 21, *mercy* (AV, RV) is *hesed*, 'devoted love', 'fidelity', such as God showed to Naomi, and Ruth to Boaz (Ru. 2:20; 3:10). The terms of this verse give content to 'filled' in Matthew 5:6.

21:22. Strategy
The truth that wisdom may succeed where brute force fails (*cf.*

24:5,6), has many applications, not least to spiritual warfare. But in this realm, earthly wisdom avails nothing: 2 Corinthians 10:4.

21:23. Least said . . .
See note on 13:3, and subject-study: Words, III, p. 48.

21:24. Portrait of the scoffer
For the words *proud* and *pride*, see on 11:2. All the terms speak of aggressive insolence; *e.g.*, *haughty* recurs in Habakkuk 2:5 (RV), of the tyrant. But *scoffer* (RSV) is the most damning, since it defines the Godward attitude. See subject-study: The Fool, III, pp. 41f.

21:25, 26. The tyranny of desire
Desire, as verb and noun, dominates these two verses, which are probably a unity. 26 begins, lit., 'All day he desires (with) desire' (as in Nu. 11:4a, Heb.); and the most natural subject of the verb is *the sluggard* (RSV) of 25. (RV's awkwardly impersonal *There is that . . .*, and RSV's conjectural *the wicked* (from LXX) are unnecessary.)

The sluggard lives in his world of wishing, which is his substitute for working. It can ruin him materially (25) and imprison him spiritually (26), for he can neither command himself nor escape himself. Contrast with this the outflowing interest and energy of the *righteous* man (26b), and notice how positive is the quality which God calls righteousness.

21:27. A sop to heaven
See the references listed at 15:8; also the subject-study: God and Man, p. 32. Line 1 already implies an unrepentant approach, therefore line 2, to go further, must allude to a cynical rather than a thoughtless attitude. The final phrase could be rendered, 'as the price of a foul deed' (*zimmâ*), an imagined bargain with God which adds insult to injury. *Cf.* Psalm 50:21. On *zimmâ*, see on 24:9.

21:28. Accurate reporting
Constantly (AV), *unchallenged* (RV), is lit. 'for ever' (12:19 explains it). The key phrase is *a man who hears*: his first aim is to know and understand, not to grind some axe. It is not without relevance to Christian 'witness': the man who listens (Is. 50:4) is the man worth listening to.

21:29. Bluff
The verb in line 2 (AV: *directeth*) means 'makes sure' (in both senses: *i.e.* of making preparation (*cf.* 31a) and of achieving stability (*cf.* 24:3b)). RSV's *considers* (LXX; a small change) weakens the contrast between the verbs. The proverb shows that a bold front is no substitute for sound principles.

21:30. 'He poureth contempt upon princes . . .'
The most succinct exposition of this is in Acts 2:23 (*cf.* Acts 4:27,28), and the fullest in 1 Corinthians 1–3. The saying can also be viewed as a complement to the motto-text of Proverbs, stating that in our outlook on life no true synthesis (*wisdom*), analysis (*understanding*, or, 'insight') or policy (*counsel*) can be arrived at in defiance of God.

21:31. '. . . and looseth the belt of the strong'
If verse 30 warns us not to fight against the Lord, 31 warns us not to fight without Him. It condemns, not earthly resources, but reliance on them: *cf.* Psalm 20:7; Isaiah 31:1–3. For two contrasted expressions of this Godward faith, study Ezra 8:22; Nehemiah 2:9.

22:1. Reputation
Our Lord carries this teaching a step further in Luke 10:20, to show that at a still higher level, not the power we wield, but the love in which we are held, is our proper joy.

22:2. Poor relations
We might have expected line 2 to read 'all go to one place', in the manner of Ecclesiastes. But it is a more significant bond that

we all come from one hand. However far ahead of the Old Testament we may think ourselves, it is hard not to be guilty of some practical denial of this truth. See also 14:31; 29:13.

22:3. Walk warily
Scripture gives blind optimism its right name: not faith, but folly. *Cf.* 14:15,16. The saying is repeated in even terser Hebrew at 27:12. *Punished* (AV): Moffatt, better, 'and pays for it'. See subject-study: Wisdom, I (4), p. 37.

22:4. They shall inherit the earth
The first Heb. word (AV: *by*; RV: *the reward of*) means 'the consequence of'. Because God is God, it just follows – but in His time. *Cf.* 21:21; Luke 14:11. (There is no *and* after *humility*; but it is probably right to supply it, rather than take the next phrase as defining 'humility', which is a harsher construction.)

22:5. The way of the transgressor
On *froward* (AV, RV), see on 2:14,15. Moffatt puts it well: 'On crooked courses men step into snares.' *Cf.* 13:15.

22:6. Formative years
The training prescribed is lit. 'according to his (the child's) way', implying, it seems, respect for his individuality and vocation, though not for his selfwill (see verse 5, or 14:12). But the stress is on parental opportunity and duty. *Train* means elsewhere to 'dedicate' a house (Dt. 20:5), temple (1 Ki. 8:63), *etc.* Possibly a trace of this meaning clings to it. See subject-study: The Family, II, pp. 50ff.

22:7. Money's leverage
An economic fact to face, but not the only one: see note on 10:15.

22:8. The furrows of unrighteousness
This is chiefly encouragement to the oppressed (see line 2). Harvest time will answer all questions. *Cf.* in general, Habakkuk 2; on sowing and reaping: Job 4:8; Hosea 8:7; 10:13; Galatians 6:7–9; Matthew 13:30.

22:9. Cheerful giver
Deuteronomy 15:9,10 and 2 Corinthians 9:7,8, answer the
objection: 'I cannot afford to be generous.' *Cf.* 19:17; 28:27.
Bountiful is lit. 'good'; *cf.* Matthew 20:15.

22:10. Troublemaker
Disagreement and bad blood sometimes arise not from the facts
of a situation but from a *person* with a wrong attitude, who makes
mischief. That is to say, what an institution sometimes needs is
not reforms, but the expulsion of a member; see Matthew 18:17.

22:11. Grace and truth
The connection between the first and second phrases is left to
the reader to supply. RSV seems right in supporting the margin
of AV, RV (*and whose speech is gracious*). It is the equal partnership
of integrity and charm, the one not diminishing the other, that
is the rarity. *Cf.* verse 29; 14:35 (and note).

22:12. Truth's guardian
RV unnecessarily alters line 1. The contrast is between truth and
falsehood, not between two kinds of men. RSV brings out the
'watchman' metaphor with its *keep watch over knowledge*. When
truth seems betrayed, here is encouragement for its friends.
(For *knowledge*, here and at 29:7 (RSV), D. W. Thomas substitutes the translation 'a lawsuit', on the basis of an Arabic
cognate noted at 24:14.[1] But 'knowledge' remains preferable.)

22:13. Lie on!
See subject-study: The Sluggard, I, p. 42, and note on 26:13–16.

22:14. The adulteress
Cf. 23:27. The subject is vividly treated in 2:16–22 and chapters
5 and 7.

22:15. Knocking the nonsense out
Foolishness (AV, RV) or *folly* (RSV) here is *'iwwelet* (see subject-
  [1] *JTS*, 1963, pp. 93f.

study: The Fool, II (2), p. 41), denoting something more positive than inexperience. *Cf.* 13:24, and subject-study: The Family, II, p. 51.

22:16. Expensive tactics

The italics in AV, RV witness to the cryptic brevity of the Hebrew. Its most natural translation is that of Delitzsch: 'Whosoever oppresseth the lowly, it is gain to him: whosoever giveth to the rich, it is only loss' – which is an ironic way of saying that you are wasting your money if you would buy a patron; more can be squeezed from the poor than wheedled from the rich. Alternatively (*cf.* verses 22, 23), Knox's rendering, through Vulg., is possible: 'Oppress the poor for thy enrichment, and ere long a richer man's claim shall impoverish thee.'

IIIa. WORDS OF WISE MEN (22:17 – 24:22)

On the character and provenance of this section of the book, see Introduction, p. 23.

22:17–21. The right use of proverbs

A series of proverbs demands much of the reader, if it is not to remain for him a string of platitudes. The present call to attention is salutary not only in its immediate context but beyond it, to enable the disciple to review his response to all Scripture. Does he read with alert concentration (17)? How much is retained and ready for passing on (18)? Does he receive it in the spirit in which it is given – to deepen his trust (19), guide his decisions (20) and strengthen his grasp of truth (21)? Does he see himself as the virtual envoy (*cf. send thee*, 21) of those whose knowledge of the truth depends on him?

20. A single word *šlšwm* is variously rendered: *heretofore* (RVmg, representing the Heb. consonants,[1] and yielding fair

---

[1] But 'heretofore' is properly a two-word expression, and the first word is missing.

sense), *excellent things* (AV, RV, using a word really meaning 'officers'; *cf.* note on 8:6), 'triply' (LXX, Vulg.; so Knox: 'not once nor twice'), *thirty sayings* (RSV). This last is the most convincing, for the section can be divided into this round number of paragraphs, and the Egyptian *Wisdom of Amenemope* (see Introduction, p. 23), which has points of contact with it, speaks of its own 'thirty chapters'.[1]

22:22, 23. Protector of the poor

The two lines of 23 mirror (and magnify) the two lines of 22: violence, litigation; litigation, violence. To be ruthlessly 'on the make' is to make, above all, an Enemy. *Cf.* 23:10,11.

22:24, 25. Bad company

See 1:10–19, and subject-study: The Friend, p. 44. *Cf. Amenemope* (see Introduction, p. 23), chapter 9:1, 2.[2]

22:26, 27. Reckless promises

See 6:1–5, and notes.

22:28. Betraying the past

While greed is the likeliest motive for such a sin (as, explicitly, in 23:10,11), here the implied stress is on its highhandedness. In Israel, land was held from God, and was inalienable (Lv. 25:23; Dt. 19:14); in every society certain heritages are similarly not the property of any one generation. But no law will protect them (*cf.* 1 Ki. 21; Is. 5:8) when integrity is absent. *Cf.* 23:10; also *Amenemope*, chapter 6:1ff.[3]

22:29. The craftsman

Anyone who puts his workmanship before his prospects towers above the thrusters and climbers of the adjacent paragraphs. *Cf.* verse 11, and note on 27:18. (*Amenemope*, chapter 30:10,11 –

---

[1] *Amenemope*, chapter 30:1; *DOTT*, p. 185.
[2] *DOTT*, p. 180.
[3] *DOTT*, p. 179.

his final saying – gives a similar assurance to the experienced scribe.[1])

23:1–8. Discomforts of the social heights
The perspiring social climber is gently chaffed, in three loosely-connected paragraphs.

1–3. How constrained and tantalized he is, even in his moment of triumph! (Amenemope (see Introduction, p. 23) in his chapter 23 recommends 'false chewings'.[2])

4, 5. Wealth is no less elusive than social prestige (translate 5a as RSV (*cf.* RVmg): *When your eyes light upon it, it is gone*); *cf.* Luke 12:20; 1 Timothy 6:7–10. *Cf.* also *Amenemope*, chapter 7:15:

> 'They have made themselves wings like geese
> And are flown away to heaven.'[3]

Similarly, from Nippur: 'Possessions are sparrows in flight which can find no place to alight.'[4]

6–8. His very skill at extracting reluctant favours only earns him secret dislike. It takes away the relish (8) (*cf. Amenemope*, chapter 11:4[5]) to have one's grudging host (*evil eye*, AV, RV: *cf.* 22:9; Mt. 20:15) doing mental arithmetic (7a) with each dish. (*Reckoneth*, 7a, RV: this translation of a rare word, supported by modern Heb., is now confirmed by Ugaritic.[6])

23:9. Wisdom wasted on a fool
In the hearing (RV, RSV): rather, *in the ears* (AV); it is direct address, not something overheard. See subject-study: The Fool, II (1), p. 40.

23:10, 11. Champion of the fatherless
Cf. 22:28 and 22:22,23. *Redeemer* is *gō'ēl*, originally the near

---

[1] *DOTT*, p. 185.
[2] *DOTT*, p. 184.
[3] *DOTT*, p. 180.
[4] *SP*, p. 50.
[5] *DOTT*, p. 181.
[6] See J. Gray, *The Legacy of Canaan*, p. 195.

kinsman who must come to the rescue of one who had fallen on hard times (*e.g.* Lv. 25:25; Ru. 3:12,13; 4:1ff.) or for the avenging of one murdered (Nu. 35:19). The term is applied to God in, *e.g.*, Genesis 48:16; Exodus 6:6; Job 19:25, and many times in Isaiah 41-63.

23:12-16. The strict school of wisdom

Godly wisdom is not lightly picked up (12; *cf.* verse 23), nor lightly imparted (13,14): the same word *mûsār* (discipline, training) is used in 12a as in 13a. The brisk 13b can be taken in two ways, and 14 underlines the second of them: the child will not only survive it, he will survive *because* of it (*cf. Ahikar*, XII, XIII[1]). But if a parent's firmness is vital, so is the child's own choice (15,16); so, too, is the underlying warmth of affection discernible in 15b, 16a. (The note of personal appeal is characteristic of this whole section, and gives it a close affinity to chapters 1-9.) With verses 22-25, this appeal binds together a man's concern for wisdom with his concern for the people he loves best. It is no private pursuit.

Reins (16, AV, RV) are kidneys. The naming of internal organs expresses the depth of an emotion (*cf.* our expressions: 'in my bones', 'in my heart of hearts', *etc.*).

23:17,18. Enviable sinners?

24:1, 19 and Psalm 37:1, 8, *etc.*, expose the simultaneous admiration and resentment which make up envy, springing from an undue preoccupation with oneself and with the present. The remedy is to look up (17b) and look ahead (18) (see also on 24:1). *Future* (18a, RSV) is better than AV or RV: see note on 5:4.

23:19-21. From revelry to rags

If Christ's enemies hoped to reinforce their attack with this scriptural ammunition (Mt. 11:19), they only made it more ludicrous, so feckless is this trifler (*cf.* 29-35) and so formidable was their actual foe.

[1] *DOTT*, p. 272.

23:22–25. A son to be proud of

Here is practical content to the fifth commandment, direct (22) and indirect (23–25). See also on verses 12–16, and subject-study: The Family, II, pp. 50ff.

23:26–28. The prostitute's clutches

Verse 26 leads into 27, 28 with special earnestness. In 26b the versions hesitate between *observe* (AV, RSV; Heb. consonants: *t-ṣ-r-n*) and *delight (in)* (RV; *t-r-ṣ-n*). The Heb. consonantal text has the latter, but it lacks a preposition – suspiciously. The Massoretes and all the ancient version were right, it would seem, to read the former, which needs no preposition.

Unchastity may be romanticized, but the hard facts are faithfully given here: captivity (27: no unaided escape), ruthlessness (28a), social disruption (28b).

23:29–35. Drink

An unforgettable study of the drunkard, as he is seen (29) and as he sees (33–35). His imagination is as uncontrollable as his legs (34); and if there is pathos in his first fascination (31), there is far more in his final bravado (35).

33. *Strange women* (AV, RVmg): rather, *strange things* (RV, RSV), as the parallel in line 2 indicates. One's senses and one's judgment can no longer be trusted.

24:1,2. Enviable sinners?

Against (AV, RV) should be simply *of* (RSV): it is the same preposition as in 23:17; 24:19. In the latter passages, the antidote to envy is the long view: the glory (23:18) or darkness (24:20) to come. Here, it is a close-up of the envied sinner, obsessed with all that is negative.

24:3,4. Founded and furnished

This constructiveness shows up well against the nihilism of verse 2. It could be literal, but is more probably symbolic, whether of the family (*cf.* 14:1), or of a man's character, or of any fine enterprise.

24:5, 6. Strategy is strength

See notes on 21:22; 11:14.

24:7. A fool out of his element

See subject-study: The Fool, II (2), p. 41. Issues of any gravity (*cf.* 5,6) quickly show up the trifler. *Wisdom* is plural here: see on 1:20 (footnote). *High* (*râmôṯ*) is spelt here with an extra but quiescent consonant, giving it the same form as the word for 'coral' in Job 28:18; Ezekiel 27:16. This has provoked some ingenious interpretations, which however are proved superfluous by the occurrence of *both* forms of spelling in the place-name Ramoth ('heights of') Gilead (Jos. 20:8; 1 Ki. 22:3). *The gate*: the equivalent of council-chamber and lawcourt.

24:8, 9. Morality flouted

Scheming is the root idea of these two proverbs, in the sense of calculated (8) and brazen (9) wickedness. (*Cf.* Moffatt, 8, 9a: 'A man who devises mischief, men call him a schemer. Now sin is folly's scheme.') Both sayings show that public opinion sooner or later condemns it. The element of brazenness in 9 is indicated both by the term *scorner* (AV, RV) and by the fact that 'scheme' (AV, RV: *thought*; Heb. *zimmâ*) often has elsewhere the special sense of 'outrage' or 'lewdness': *e.g.* Leviticus 18:17c; Judges 20:6. So much for the 'freethinker'.

24:10–12. The quitter

Exceptional strain (10) and avoidable responsibility (11, 12) are fair tests, not unfair, of a man's mettle. It is the hireling, not the true shepherd, who will plead bad conditions (10), hopeless tasks (11) and pardonable ignorance (12); love is not so lightly quieted – nor is the God of love.

11. See also note on 28:17. RSV translates 11b well: ... *stumbling to the slaughter*. G. R. Driver,[1] however, adduces an Aramaic root to support '. . . at the point of' as against 'stumbling to'.

---

[1] *ZAW*, 1934, p. 146.

24:13, 14. Pleasure with profit

Both verses open with imperatives in the Heb. Since that of 14 has unusual vowels, it may derive not from *y-d-'* (*know*) but from a conjectured *d-'-h* ('seek').[1] This would lead well into line 2: 'So seek wisdom for your soul; if you find it . . .' On *a reward* (AV, RV), or *a future* (RSV), *cf.* note on 5:4.

24:15, 16. Resilience of the righteous

This appeal is to the only thing a wicked man consults: his interests. At a more modest level it is a salutary reminder that an unscrupulous victory is never permanent: you are fighting against God.

24:17, 18. Never gloat

Verse 18 shows that 17 is far from optional, for the point of 18b is that your glee may well be a more punishable sin than all the guilt of your enemy. A comparable warning appears in Romans 11:18–21, and an ancient parallel to verse 17 in *The Words of Ahikar*, VII.[2]

(Some commentators, however (*e.g.* Oesterley), interpret 18 as malicious: *i.e.*, 'do nothing to arouse God's pity for him.' But apart from the disharmony of this with the teaching of, *e.g.*, verse 29, or 25:21,22, it involves a glaring self-contradiction, since the proverb (on this view) seeks the success of the very animosity which it discourages.)

24:19, 20. Never envy sinners

See verse 1, and note.

24:21, 22. The godly citizen

1 Peter 2:17 uses 21a to clinch the teaching that good citizenship is part of godliness; *cf.* Romans 13:1–7, where verse 4 chimes in with our verse 22.

Some details are uncertain, but the over-all teaching is clear. For *them that are given to change* (AV, RV; *šônîm*) LXX supports the

---

[1] Inferred from an Arabic parallel: D. W. Thomas, *JTS*, 1937, p. 401.
[2] *DOTT*, p. 271.

reading *either of them* (*šᵉnêhem*; so RSV), in which case *their calamity* (*etc.*) is the calamity which they inflict. This makes sense of the final *of them both*, which is obscure in AV, RV. But a similar construction can be kept without altering the Heb., if we understand *šônîm* to mean 'those of exalted rank'.[1]

IIIb. FURTHER WORDS OF WISE MEN (24:23–34)

24:23–26. Straight speaking
Note the paradox, that a proper forthrightness, costly though it may seem, wins gratitude, and (26) has its special charm. *Cf.* Knox's 26, freely: 'The right word spoken seals all, like a kiss on the lips.' See also 25:11,12, and subject-study: Words, III (a), p. 48.

24:27. Foundations for the home
The housebuilding probably means the founding of a family (*cf.* 14:1): a matter that must wait its turn till *afterwards*. As, in a rural economy, well-worked fields justify and nourish the farm-house, so a well-ordered life (in things material and immaterial) should be established before marriage.

24:28. Groundless accusation
The second line (lit. 'and wilt thou deceive . . .?') shows that the proverb is aimed not at the mere busybody (as 3:30; 25:8–10) but at the false accuser, that abomination to God (6:19) and to the law (Dt. 19:18–21). See also references at 14:5.

24:29. Vengefulness
See on 20:22; *cf.* Romans 12:19. *Amenemope*, 2:18ff. has a fine saying to this effect; see Introduction, p. 23.

24:30–34. The sluggard overwhelmed
Cf. 6:6–11; see subject-study: The Sluggard, p. 43.

[1] On an Arabic and Syriac analogy, supported by Ugaritic, see D. W. Thomas, *ZAW*, 1934, p. 236; 1935, p. 207.

IV. FURTHER PROVERBS OF SOLOMON
(HEZEKIAH'S COLLECTION) (25:1 – 29:27)

25:1. Title
See Introduction, p. 22.

25:2–7. Kings and courtiers (cf. 16:10 – 15)
2–5. The glory of kings. Verse 2 appropriately opens Hezekiah's collection, for he was exemplifying the maxim by his enquiring zeal. But it is chiefly praising not academic research but administrative probes: the king should know what is going on.

Mystery has its place, and the autocrat knows how to keep his counsel (3); but mystery also shelters the worthless and breeds corruption (4,5) (5b repeats 16:12b). An evil harboured is even more unsettling than an evil exposed.

6, 7. Promotion at court. This direct social advice is turned by Jesus into a parable (Lk. 14:7–10) of our whole attitude to life.

The last phrase of 7 is translated by LXX, Symmachus, Vulg., *what your eyes have seen*, and attached by the last two and many moderns (*e.g.* RSV) to verse 8, where see note. This is probably right, since 7c is otherwise an extra flourish, out of place in a sequence where brevity reigns.

25:8–10. Is your tale true – kind – necessary?
The last phrase of 7 (see note) should probably introduce 8a, with the consonants of the latter revocalized, to read: *What your eyes have seen, do not hastily bring into court* (RSV).

The healthy directness advocated in 9a (*cf.* verses 11,12) is doubly wise: one seldom knows the full facts, or interprets them perfectly (8); and one's motives in spreading a story are seldom as pure as one pretends (10). To run to the law or to the neighbours is usually to run away from the duty of personal relationship – see Christ's clinching comment in Matthew 18:15b.

(Our Lord also turns the whole subject of out-of-court settlement into a parable of the fleeting day of grace: Matthew 5:25,26.)

25:11, 12. Finely said, finely taken
The directness of 9a need not be heavy-handed; *cf.* 24:26, and our Lord's artistry. But in the end the recipient is the one adorned (12), for reproof is one of the few things more blessed to receive than to give.

Apples: the word indicates some fruit known for its scent (apple, quince?).

Gold: possibly, in 11, the colour (indicating oranges, apricots?); more probably the material, as in 12.

Pictures (AV), *Baskets* (RV): the word elsewhere suggests designs (immaterial, 18:11b; or material, Lv. 26:1b), therefore RSV's *a setting* seems appropriate.

The whole simile is of uncertain interpretation, but at least its components (with those of 12) carry associations of attractiveness, value and craftsmanship.

25:13. Refreshing faithfulness
There is a pungent contrast in 26:6; see also (on messengers) 13:17, and (on refreshment) 25:25.

25:14. The big talker
The *gift* is a present, not a talent; so RSV: . . . *who boasts of a gift he does not give*. It applies above all to false teachers (Jude 12 alludes to it) who win followers by promises that never materialize (*cf.* 2 Pet. 2:19).

25:15. Quiet persistence
'One does not show forbearance to a prince', objects Toy. But the quality that is praised is a refusal to be provoked, and the point is that so unassuming a weapon may win surprising victories (*cf.* line 2; also, *e.g.*, 1 Sa. 24:17; 1 Pet. 3:15,16). See also 15:1; 16:14,32.

25:16. Knowing when to stop

A parable of the fatal difference between healthy appetite and greed. Since Eden, man has wanted the last ounce out of life, as though beyond God's 'enough' lay ecstasy, not nausea. See also verse 27.

25:17. Knowing when to go

This saying, like verse 16, pivots on the word 'sated' (lit. '. . . lest he be sated with you'). It is not the only proverb to enjoin the good manners which embody a consideration for people's feelings and convenience. *Cf.* verse 20, and see subject-study: The Friend, 1 (*b*) 4, p. 45. *Withdraw* (AV) is lit. 'make rare'. A close parallel to this saying is found in *Ahikar*, XXXII.[1]

25:18. False witness

See references listed at 14:5.

25:19. Confidence misplaced

The Heb. allows us to understand the unfaithful man to be either the one trusted or the one trusting. Each makes excellent sense, but the use of the word *confidence* (AV, RV) elsewhere tends to support the latter interpretation (*cf.* Moffatt, against AV, RV, RSV): see especially Job 8:13–15.

25:20. Heartless jollity

'Soda' is nearer the Heb. *neṭer* than is *nitre* (AV, RV). To pour acid on this alkali is 'first of all to make it effervesce, and, secondly, to destroy its specific qualities' (Martin). In another context this could suggest a beneficial stimulus or counteraction, but here it must indicate provocation or incongruity. LXX has a simpler simile (see RSV, Moffatt): 'as vinegar on a sore', which *may* show that the Heb. originally read *neṭeq* (scab); but *neṭeq* hardly suggests anything sufficiently sensitive to give point to the proverb.

See subject-study: The Friend, 1 (*b*) 4, p. 45; *cf.* Romans 12:15.

[1] *DOTT*, p. 273.

25:21, 22. The best revenge
This saying is the topmost of a cluster of peaks (see 24:11,12, 17,18,29) which are all outcrops of an underlying care for others and faith in God presupposed throughout the book. The *coals of fire* represent the pangs which are far better felt now as shame than later as punishment (Ps. 140:10). *Cf. Amenemope*, chapter 2:19ff. (see Introduction, p. 23).

25:23. Chill wind of slander
AV's *driveth away rain*, which follows Symmachus, Vulg., and Jewish commentators, is supported by geography and by the Heb. word-order in line 2. But this order is not decisive, and 'driveth away' is a wishful translation: the word normally means *bringeth forth*, as in RV, RSV. So Moffatt: 'North winds bring rain: slander brings angry looks.' Since, however, in Palestine the north is noted for dry weather, it is hard to account for such a simile. Of the suggested solutions[1] perhaps the best is B. Gemser's, that the saying originated outside Palestine (*cf.* Ec. 12:9b, and Introduction, pp. 25f.)

25:24. The scold
See note on the identical 21:9.

25:25. Suspense and relief
The point of this *far country* is that it contains someone from home, news of whom (and help for whom) can only be scarce and slow. In the spiritual realm, as in the natural, love is open to this tantalization, and to a corresponding joy. (See 1 Thes. 3:5-8; 2 Cor. 7:5-7; Lk. 15:13; and references at note on Pr. 15:30.) For the simile, *cf.* verse 13 and Jeremiah 18:14.

25:26. The spreading poison of compromise
Follow RSV here: *Like a muddied spring or a polluted fountain is a righteous man who gives way before the wicked.* For *muddied*, *cf.* Ezekiel 34:18,19. Here it is a most telling comparison, since a good man's defection imperils, or at best deprives, the many

[1] *Cf.* J. van der Ploeg, *VT*, 1953, pp. 189f. for some of these.

who have learnt to rely on him. The stream still flows; the name still reassures.

25:27. Too much of a good thing
With line 1, *cf.* verse 16. In line 2, the insertion of *not* in AV, RV seems a desperate expedient, although admittedly a negative in one clause can extend its influence into a second that closely matches it (*e.g.* Nu. 23:19a, Heb., and other examples listed in Gesenius §152z; but none is as harsh as the present one).

RSV makes a mosaic from fragments of ancient versions. Less precariously, the traditional vowels can be altered to yield either (a) 'But the study of difficult things is honour' (Delitzsch and others), or (b) 'And he who despises honour is honoured' (D. W. Thomas[1]). The former leaves the consonants intact, but follows line 1 rather abruptly; the latter changes the word-division, omits one consonant, and assumes the meaning 'despises', on the strength of an Arabic root (perhaps supported by 28:11). This arrives at a similar sense to that of AV, RV, which still seems the most suitable conclusion to the verse, though the route must remain debatable.

25:28. Soft victim
Impatience views restraint only as restriction; so the enemy arrives to find the walls down. For the converse, see 16:32.

26:1–12. Mostly about fools
See subject-study: The Fool, II (1), p. 40.

1. The fool promoted (i). *Cf.* verse 8. *Rain in harvest* suggests that damage, not only incongruity, comes of capricious evaluations. (The present age, through the tricks of publicity, is especially prone to idolize 'vain and light persons', for whom the treatment of verse 3 might be better medicine. See note on 19:10.)

2. The answer to superstition. RSV: *Like a sparrow in its flitting, like a swallow in its flying, a curse that is causeless does not alight*. By its picture of random flight, the proverb scouts the

[1] *JTS*, Oct. 1937, pp. 402ff.

idea of a curse speeding to its target like a magic arrow, regardless of justice. Balaam is the reluctant witness against all superstition: 'How can I curse whom God has not cursed?' (Nu. 23:8, RSV).

3. Handling the fool. Psalm 32:9 should warn us that this proverb, with its fellows, is written for us in two capacities: as people dealing with fools, and as potential fools ourselves. Those who invite the rod are those who contrive to ignore the glance: Psalm 32:8.

4, 5. Answering the fool. These twin sayings, which would have invited the charge of inconsistency had they not stood together (and did incur it, even so, from some Rabbis, who thereupon questioned the canonicity of the book), bring out the dilemma of those who would reason with the unreasonable. *Cf.* 2 Corinthians 12:11, and 11:16 leading up to it, where Paul found himself talking as a fool (*cf.* our verse 4b), yet knew that a refusal to use their terms would have confirmed his foolish flock in their opinions (*cf.* our verse 5b).

6. The fool as messenger. For the converse, see 25:13.

7. The fool as philosopher (i). *Cf.* 9, and subject-study: The Fool, II (1), p. 40. The predicate in line 1 (a single verb, *dalyû*) is elusive. The verb means to draw water out of a well (*cf.* 20:5), which has provoked many conjectures. Delitzsch takes it to suggest dangling (as of a bucket on a rope), and this approximates to most modern translations which presuppose a copyist's error for *dallû* ('hang limp'). Knox renders the Vulg. engagingly: 'Give a fool leave to speak, it is all fair legs and no walking.'

8. The fool promoted (ii). *Cf.* verse 1. RSV (*like one who binds the stone in the sling*) supports AV and RVmg against RV. That is to say, the procedure is nonsensical, for the stone is there to be slung out. So is the fool.

9. The fool as philosopher (ii). *Cf.* 7. Moffatt has: 'Like thorny branches brandished by a drunkard.' Contrast with this the shrewd handling proper to these pointed sayings: Ecclesiastes 12:11.

10. The fool as employee (?). The text seems damaged

beyond repair. Since several of the words have more than one meaning, numerous combinations have been tried, none of them self-authenticating. In line 1, *raḇ* may mean 'archer', or 'much', or 'great one'; and *meḥôlēl*: 'wounding' or 'bringing forth'. Line 2 seems to mean that a fool and a casual labourer make equally poor employees (but RSV's *drunkard*, from the Syriac, represents a more convincing way of vocalizing the consonants of the second *he that hireth*, as RV).

11. The confirmed fool. 2 Peter 2:22 quotes this to show that by this action such a person gives himself away. Not his sampling of better things, but his reversion to the lower, is the test of him – just as the tastes that a dog does *not* share with man stamp him as unmistakably dog. See, in the light of this, Hebrews 6:4–8; 1 John 2:19.

12. The fool surpassed. The second line shows that this man is no dunce. While the fool pilloried in Proverbs is an opinionated creature (23:9), his stupidity may at least earn him a lesson (26:3). There is more, however, for an abler man's vanity to feed on, and more damage that he can do (*cf.* 29:20). See 1 Corinthians 3:18; 8:2.

26:13–16. The sluggard

See the subject-study, p. 42. Admiration for the wit of this portraiture has to be tempered with disquiet, on reflection that the sluggard will be the last to see his own features here (see 16), for he has no idea that he is lazy: he is not a shirker but a 'realist' (13); not self-indulgent but 'below his best in the morning' (14); his inertia is 'an objection to being hustled' (15); his mental indolence a fine 'sticking to his guns' (16).

26:17–28. Mischief-making

17. Interference. *Passeth by* may qualify either the busybody (AV, RV; emphasizing the intrusion), or the dog (RSV; emphasizing the risk). While *meddles* (AV, RSV) makes excellent sense, and is supported by Vulg., Syr., it is most easily derived from the root *'-r-b*, as against the Heb. text's root *'-b-r* ('gets angry', *cf.* RV), which scarcely calls for improvement.

18, 19. Misleading jests. Proverbs, with its emphasis on the duty of forethought, does not countenance escape-clauses (19b; *cf.* 24:12a), least of all the plea: 'I meant no harm, I never thought . . .'. *Cf.* subject-study: The Friend, 1 (*b*), p. 45.

20–28. Malicious talk. The various aspects of this evil give rise to various pictures:

20, 21. COALS. It is the whisperer or quarreller himself, not (as he would claim) the truth, that feeds the fires; for his mind refashions facts into fuel.

22. TITBITS. See note on 18:8, and subject-study: Words, 1 (1), p. 46.

23–26. GLAZE. Verses 24–26 enlarge on 23's simile of surface and substratum. The contrast is not between costly (*silver*) and cheap, but between smooth and rough, or shining and sombre. The puzzle of *silver dross* (AV, RV; *kesep̄ sîḡîm*) has found its probable solution through a text from Ras Shamra, on the basis of which H. L. Ginsberg suggests re-pointing the consonants to read *kᵉsap̄sāḡîm*: 'like glaze' (*cf.* RSV).[1]

27. THE TRAP. In the present context, *i.e.*, reinforcing the assurance of 26, this metaphor shows how insincerity of speech recoils upon its perpetrator. It is used in a more general sense in *e.g.* 28:10; Psalm 7:15; *cf. The Words of Ahikar*, XXXVIII.[2]

28. The heart of the matter (20–28) is exposed in 28, with the fact that deceit, whether it hurts or soothes, is practical hatred, since truth is vital, and pride fatal, to right decisions. Contrast 27:6.

27:1. Boasting of tomorrow

James 4:13–16 enlarges on this, and Matthew 6:34 (19–34) on the companion sin of worry. Both are rectified by an embracing of the present will of God: *cf.* Psalm 37:3.

27:2. Boasting of oneself

The New Testament carries this still further: John 12:43. Only *God's* praise cannot be angled for, and cannot corrupt.

---

1 See *WIANE*, p. 12; *DOTT*, p. 127, n. 19.
2 *DOTT*, p. 274.

27:3. A fool's anger
See subject-study: The Fool, II (2), p. 41. RSV's *a fool's provocation* is possible (Dt. 32:19,27) and appropriate, but a less common construction than that of AV, RV.

27:4. Jealousy
See 6:32–35; Song of Solomon 8:6,7. Jealousy in Scripture is seldom (but see 14:30) the unhealthy jealousy-*of*; normally it is jealousy-*for*; *i.e.*, it is a proper intolerance of disruptive intrusion, and is thereby a mark of love (as the opposite of indifference). See also Exodus 20:5; 1 Kings 19:10; Zechariah 8:2.

27:5, 6. Frankness between friends
Cf. 28:23; 29:5; and subject-study: The Friend, I (*b*), p. 45.
    Hidden (5, RV, RSV): *i.e.*, a love 'manifesting itself by no rebuking word, and therefore morally useless; or, by a change of vowels, *love that conceals*, that is, does not tell the friend his faults' (Toy).
    Profuse (6b, RV, RSV): the AV's and Vulg.'s *deceitful* makes a more direct contrast, but is hard to justify linguistically. G. R. Driver[1] argues for 'brazen', from an Arabic root. Other suggestions ('corrupting', 'like razors', *etc.*) all involve slight changes in the Heb. consonants.

27:7. Unenviable repletion
This is not a truism about food, but a parable about possessions. It bears on (among other things) the disposition we acquire by the level of comfort we choose. A bilious outlook is a poor prize.

27:8. The wanderer
The thought is not so much of homelessness (the nest is built for the brood) as of a deserted charge and a forfeited hope of a posterity. (Note *her* (AV, RV) – it is the mother bird.) It condemns, by implication, the 'rolling stone', not the fugitive (1 Sa. 26:19) nor the pilgrim (Heb. 11:13,14).

[1] *JTS*, 1940, p. 175.

27:9. 'Sweet counsel together'

The Heb. of line 2 is awkward (lit. 'and his friend's sweetness from counsel of soul'), and the suggested renderings are many. LXX (with a different text), followed by RSV, makes a lame contrast between perfume and trouble. Without changing the consonants, G. R. Driver reads, 'one's friend is sweeter than fragrant trees.'[1] Others take the last phrase to mean 'is better than one's own counsel'. But AV, RV get the closest link with the first line, and the fullest meaning. See also subject-study: The Friend, 1 (*b*) 3, p. 45.

27:10. The old family friend

The *brother* is mentioned, not to decry his help but to emphasize that of a tested friend, by so high a comparison (*cf.* 18:24). To insert the word 'even' before 'to thy brother's house', would clarify the point. See subject-study: The Friend, 1 (*b*) 1, p. 45. There is an exact parallel to the final clause in *The Words of Ahikar*, XIX.[2]

27:11. The teacher's joy

Cf. 10:1, and references there. For this eager concern *cf.* 1 Thessalonians 2:19,20; 3:8.

27:12. Walk warily

See 22:3.

27:13. Hostage to fortune

This is a near-repetition of 20:16, where see note. On standing surety, see on 6:1-5.

27:14. Fatuous friend

On such abuses of goodwill, *cf.* 26:18,19, and subject-study: The Friend, 1 (*b*) 4, p. 45. It matters not only *what* we say, but *how*, *when* and *why* we say it.

---

[1] *ZAW*, 1934, p. 54.
[2] *DOTT*, p. 273.

27:15, 16. Nagging wife

See on 19:13. In 16, AV's construction is forced. Follow RSV: *to restrain her is to restrain the wind, or to grasp oil in his right hand.* (*Restrain* is, in spite of Toy (*ICC*), a legitimate translation as Hosea 13:12 shows ('kept in store', like a ledger under lock and key)[1] and *grasp* expresses the purpose of the movement which (lit.) *encountereth* (RV) nothing but oil.)

In other words, you are dealing with someone 'as unsteady as the wind, and as slippery as oil' (Fritsch); you will never tie such a person down.

27:17. Stimulating contact

Countenance (AV, RV) almost equals 'personality' here. Like 'soul', it can stand for the man himself (*cf.* RSV). See subject-study: The Friend, 1 (*b*)3, p. 45.

27:18. Rewards of service

Moffatt brings out the correspondence between the two verbs: 'He who tends . . .; he who attends to . . .'. *Cf.* 2 Timothy 2:6,15. The unsuccessful servant may affect to despise honours; but the 'place-hunter' and the 'favourite' are sometimes none other than the whole-hearted as seen by the half-hearted. *Cf.* 22:29.

27:19. Self-knowledge

The Heb. is very cryptic: lit., 'As the water the face to the face, so the man's heart to the man.' This may mean: 'if you would see yourself, look within – not in the mirror.' Alternatively, the second line could mean: 'so is one man's heart to another' – *i.e.* just as a mirror confronts you with your public shape, so your fellow man confronts you with the shape in which thoughts and habits like your own have grouped themselves into a character.

27:20. Never satisfied

On *Sheol and Abaddon* (RV, RSV), see note on 15:11; for their insatiability, *cf.* 30:15,16; Isaiah 5:14; Habakkuk 2:5. Fallen

[1] *Cf.* G. R. Driver, *JTS*, 1940, p. 175.

man's restlessness (*cf.* Ec. 1:8) is assuaged in Christ: John 4:13,14; Philippians 4:11-13.

27:21. The crucible
The second line in 17:3 runs 'But the Lord trieth the hearts'. The present proverb shows one of His processes (*and a man is* (*tried*) *by his praise*, RV), possibly the most searching of all. The proportions of praise meted out to Saul and David in 1 Samuel 18:7 threw both men into the crucible. *Cf.* Jn. 12:42,43.

Alternative interpretations are: (a) that we stand revealed by what *we* praise (RVmg); (b) that reputation is a fair guide to worth. But the crucible is for refining and preparing the metal, not for mere analysis.

27:22. Ingrained folly
The folly that is rejection of 'the beginning of wisdom' is no isolated trait: it must colour the whole character. See subject-study: The Fool, II (2), p. 41.

Bray (AV, RV): *i.e.*, pound. The Heb. for *mortar* is the noun from this verb, *i.e.*, a pounding-bowl.

27:23-27. Pastoral symphony
This country scene is not designed to make farmers of everybody, but to show the proper interplay of man's labour and God's nurture, which a sophisticated society neglects at its peril. It recalls the reader from the scramble for money and position (24) to the satisfaction of doing a worth-while job well (23), and to a recognition of the rhythm (25) and sufficiency (26,27) of God's care.

28:1. 'Where no fear was' (Ps. 53:5)
Bold: 'confident' is nearer the meaning. The straightforward man, like the lion, has no need to look over his shoulder. What is at his heels is not his past (Nu. 32:23) but his rearguard: God's goodness and mercy (Ps. 23:6).

28:2. The scramble for power
In just over two centuries, northern Israel, for its sins, had nine

dynasties, each, after the first, inaugurated by an assassination (see God's comments in Ho. 7:7; 8:4; 13:11). In three and a half centuries, Judah, for David's sake, had only one. *State* (AV, RV): better, *stability* (RSV).

28:3. Unnatural tyrant
Some are inclined to read, with LXX, 'wicked' (Heb. *rāšā'*), as in 15, instead of *poor* (*rāš*), on the ground that the tyrant's circumstances are immaterial. But this tyranny has the double bitterness of betrayal (by one who should have had fellow-feeling) and squalor (for it is worse to suffer under a Jehoiakim, where all is in decline, than under a Solomon). It is well compared with the calamity of the freakish rain that brings havoc instead of blessing. The proverb has a down-to-earth relevance, since it is this drab oppression which will alone be within the power of most of its hearers to exercise.

28:4. God's law man's bastion
Without revelation, all is soon relative; and with moral relativity, nothing quite merits attack. So, *e.g.*, the tyrant is accepted because he gets things done; and the pervert, because his condition is interesting. The full sequence appears in Romans 1:18-32.

28:5. God's law man's light
Romans 1:21,28 illuminates line 1, as Romans 1:18-32 the preceding proverb. On line 2, *cf.* Psalm 119:100; John 7:17, and other references given in RVmg.

28:6. How much is he worth?
See on 19:1. *Ways*, here and in 18, is in the dual number, intensifying the idea of double-dealing which is already present in *perverse* or, better, 'crooked'.

28:7. A son to be proud of
This distils the essence of the eloquent 23:19-25.

28:8. The extortioner's estate

The process, if usually slow, is as sure as the promise, 'The meek shall inherit the earth.' *Cf.*, in the shorter run, the Canaanites' 'great and goodly cities' destined for Israel.

Usury or (RSV) *interest*: the Mosaic law shows that the legitimacy of it depends on its context: what was quite proper in terms of economics (Dt. 23:20) was pronounced improper in terms of family care (Dt. 23:19) – as if a doctor should charge for treating his own children.

28:9. Prayer as insult

So much for religious exercises as a sop to conscience. See references at 15:8.

28:10. Corruption of others

This attracted some of Christ's strongest words: see Matthew 5:19; 18:6; 23:15. Its motivation varies: *e.g.* hatred of a high standard (Am. 2:12); pride in one's opinions (Col. 2:18); a desire to dominate (2 Tim. 3:6). What is constant is the readiness to use other people as means to one's own ends (*cf.* 2 Pet. 2:15,18).

On falling into one's own pit, *cf.* 26:27.

28:11. Pretentiousness seen through

God's searching gaze, as prayed for in Psalm 139:23, may have to reach a man in the unwelcome form of the appraising (or contemptuous? – see on 25:27) stare of one whom he regards as an inferior. Three things are implied in the saying: (a) wisdom is no respecter of rank; (b) complacency is no symptom of wisdom; (c) a man's peers are not always his best judges.

28:12. A people's happiness

The theme recurs in verse 28 and in 29:2. See note on 11:10.

Rejoice (AV): *i.e.*, have cause to rejoice; so RV, RSV: *triumph*. *Hidden* (AV): lit. 'will (*i.e.* must?) be searched for'. *Cf.* Amos 5:13.

28:13. Sin buried is sin kept

The classic Old Testament expansion of line 1 is Psalm 32:1–4; and of line 2, the rest of the psalm. In the New Testament: 1 John 1:6–9.

28:14. 'Rejoice with trembling'

Feareth: the Heb. uses a strengthened form of a strong word: *i.e.* 'is in great awe', in contrast with the brazenness of line 2. Philippians 2:12–18 testifies to the happiness that blossoms from so unpromising a stem.

28:15, 16. Mindless tyranny

The reproach implicit in the comparison with wild beasts is explicit in 16. The tyrant is in God's eyes subhuman (15), stupid (16a) and shortlived (16b). *Cf.* the unflattering historical pageant in Daniel 7:1–8, and the quiet irony of our Lord in Luke 22:24,25.

28:17. The murderer

The first phrase cannot be active (as AV); the verb means 'oppressed', hence RV, RSV *laden, burdened*, although elsewhere it always refers to objective oppression. The proverb states that the offender himself (like the smitten Azariah, 2 Ch. 26:20) hastens to his punishment, once his conscience is awake. 24:11,12 must be taken in conjunction with this proverb (as Delitzsch points out); the former forbids indifference to suffering; the latter forbids interference with justice. *Cf.* Numbers 35:31.

28:18. Nothing to hide, nothing to fear

See the companion proverb, 10:9. *At once* (AV, RV) is lit. 'in one'; *i.e.*, either at one blow, or, in one of the 'two ways' (see note on verse 6) which he is trying to combine.

28:19. The diligent and the dilettante

RSV (*plenty of bread . . . plenty of poverty*) brings out the matching phrases concealed by AV, RV. A less symmetrical version is found at 12:11.

28:20. What is he worth?
God answers this question not in man's sense; and His is the last word. *Cf.* verse 22, and references at 20:21.

28:21. Favouritism
At 18:5 the stress is on the injustice to others; here, on the self-demeaning of the judge. *Cf.* Moffatt, freely: '– to sin, bribed by a bit of bread!' The price can go still lower, to as little as the fancied approval of a stronger personality; and the preacher (Ezk. 13:19) is as vulnerable as the judge.

28:22. Miser's miscalculation
A grudging or grasping spirit (*evil eye*, AV, RV: *cf.* 23:6; Mt. 20:15) ensures inner poverty (*cf.* 25 and 27), even while the outer hoard lasts. See also verse 20.

28:23. Welcome outspokenness
Cf. 27:5,6; 29:5. The Heb. for *afterwards* (ah^aray) is puzzling. (a) It looks like 'after me' (*i.e.* 'as I instruct'), but the personal note intrudes abruptly. (b) It may be a rare adverbial form (*cf. māṭay*). (c) G. R. Driver makes it an adjective cognate to Babylonian *ahurru*, 'common man': *i.e.* 'as a rebuker an ordinary man shall find ...'.[1] This is ingenious, but the common man hardly seems called for. Other suggestions involve emendations.

28:24. Inhuman son
Knox: 'Shall he who robs father or mother make light of it? He is next door to a murderer.' Jesus showed that there are refined ways of incurring this guilt (Mk. 7:11); *cf.* Paul's strong words in 1 Timothy 5:4,8.

28:25. 'Seek ye first ...'
On the first line (reading *greedy*, RV, RSV), see on verse 22. Line 2 puts the positive side, which is developed in Matthew 6:19-34.

[1] *ZAW*, 1934, p. 147.

28:26. Walk in wisdom
Placed here, line 1 gains force from 25b. *Wisely* (AV, RV) is *in wisdom* (RSV); the contrast with line 1 shows clearly that such wisdom is (as always in Proverbs) God-taught.

28:27. The blessedness of giving
See, among many on this theme, 22:9, and the cluster in 11:24–26.

28:28. A people's dismay
A companion to verse 12 and 29:2; see note on 11:10.

29:1. Beyond reform
This theme is presented dramatically in Jeremiah 19:10,11, and its warning enlarged upon in Proverbs 1:24–33.

29:2. A people's happiness
Cf. 28:12,28; 29:16. The first verb of line 1 ('increase') chimes with 28:28; 29:16, and yields good sense. AV and RSV gratuitously alter a Heb. consonant to enforce a stricter parallel (*are in authority*) with line 2.

29:3. A father's joy
See 28:7, and note on 10:1.

29:4. A country's stability
Line 2 begins, lit., 'But a man of offerings': *i.e.* one whose interest lies there. See verse 14, and note on 15:27.

29:5. Flattery
Cf. 28:23, and subject-study: Words, 1 (1), p. 46.

29:6. Sin's entanglement
Knox supplies the implicit comparison: 'innocence goes singing and rejoicing on its way.' Probably we should follow one Heb. MS which has: 'the righteous runs (*yārûṣ* for *yārûn*) and rejoices', since (a) Proverbs seldom duplicates an expression

(sing, rejoice); (b) the form *yārûn* is irregular; (c) the first line seems to require a contrasting figure of movement in the second.

29:7. Care for the unprivileged
Knows and *knowledge* (RSV) refer to the personal concern which makes the verb 'to know' far richer in Heb. than in English. Line 2 (lit. '. . . . understandeth not knowledge') is well interpreted by RSV's insertion of *such* before *knowledge*. A fine example of such care is seen in Job 29:12–17. (See also note at 22:12.)

29:8. Troublemakers, peacemakers
Scornful (AV, RV) refers to spiritual (rather than social) arrogance. AV's *bring . . . into a snare* should rather be 'inflame' (*cf.* RV, RSV): the fanning of party strife which brings a quick sense of power, while 'peaceable wisdom' must work and wait (see Jas. 3:13–18).

29:9. Controversy with a fool
The general sense is clear: there is no arguing calmly with a fool. But it is uncertain whether the subject of line 2 is the wise man (whose tactics are all unavailing) or, as seems more probable, the fool (who will adopt any approach but the quietly objective).

29:10. Good men persecuted
As against AV's obscurity and RSV's emendation, RV makes the best sense of line 2 (*and as for the upright, they seek his life*), for to seek a man's life (or, soul) is regularly a hostile expression in the Old Testament, as *e.g.* 1 Kings 19:10. The mixture of plural (*the upright*) and singular (*his*) means in Heb. idiom 'every single one'. *Cf.* John 15:18ff.

29:11. Self-control
His mind (AV) is lit. 'his spirit', *i.e.*, from the context, *his anger* (RV, RSV). Line 2 is lit. 'but a wise man calms it back'. If the adverb indicates repression, the verb (used in Ps. 89:9 (Heb., 10)

of the stilling of a storm) speaks of anger overcome, not merely checked. See also 14:17, 29; 16:32; 25:28.

29:12. False master, false men

'They are so because they deceive him, and they become so; for instead of saying the truth which the ruler does not wish to hear, they seek to gain his favour by deceitful flatteries, misrepresentations, exaggerations, falsehoods' (Delitzsch).

29:13. One sky over all

To this reminder of common blessings, 22:2 adds that of a common origin, and Job 3:19 of a common departure. Jesus, in Matthew 5:44,45, goes beyond the social implications of this saying, to the spiritual, by placing His followers at the giving end, as well as the receiving end, of such a process.

29:14. The king who wins loyalty

Cf. verse 4; and 16:12. The test of a man in power, and his hidden strength, is the extent to which he keeps faith with those who can put least pressure on him.

29:15. Rod and reproof

Cf. 17, and subject-study: The Family, II, p. 51.

29:16. Evil outlived

See on verse 2, and references there. This saying carries the theme further than its companions by its closing assurance. *Cf.* Habakkuk 2:2-4,12-14.

29:17. Through discipline to delight

Cf. 15, and subject-study: The Family, II, p. 51.

29:18. No vision

Vision (AV, RV) is to be taken in its exact sense of the revelation a prophet receives. *Law* in line 2 is its complement. 'The law, the prophets and the wisdom literature meet in this verse' (*The New Bible Commentary*). *Perish* (AV): rather, 'run wild'. The verb means to let loose, *e.g.* to let one's hair down, whether literally (Lv. 13:45; Nu. 5:18; ?Jdg. 5:2) or figuratively (especially Ex. 32:25 (twice): RV 'broken loose', *etc.*). This latter verse is perhaps the intended background to the proverb, with its contrast between the glory on the mountain of vision and law, and the shame in the valley. 1 Samuel 3:1, with its context, also exemplifies the saying, in showing the dependence of public morality on the knowledge of God.

29:19. Stubborn servant

This apparently sweeping statement (*cf.* 21) is seen, when balanced by others (*e.g.* 17:2), to refer to the slave *mentality*, unresponsive, irresponsible. A good servant will rise above it, whatever his status: *cf.*, on the literal level, 1 Timothy 6:1, 2; on the spiritual level, John 15:14,15; Galatians 4:7 with Philippians 1:1; Psalm 32:9.

29:20. The fool outclassed

On the unfavourable comparison see note on 26:12; also subject-study: Words, III, p. 48.

29:21. Pampered servant

While this is clearly a warning to the indulgent master, its precise prediction eludes us because of a rare final word, *mānôn*. The ancient versions make plausible guesses (*e.g.* Vulg. *contumax*, whence Knox: 'Pamper thy slave young, and breed a pert manservant'). AV, RV, RSV derive *mānôn* from the root *nîn* or *nûn*, 'to have offspring'. D. W. Thomas suggests vocalizing it as *mānûn*, 'a weakling', from a possible root *m-n-n* akin to a common Arabic word 'to be, or make, weak'.[1] The word recurs in Ecclesiasticus 47:23, of Rehoboam.

On the ways of servants, *cf.* 19 (and note); 17:2; 19:10; 25:13; 30:10,22,23.

---

[1] J. Reider, apparently independently, makes the same suggestion in *VT*, 1954, pp. 285f.

29:22. Storm-centre

Angry and *wrathful* (RV) describe the general disposition here, not a temporary state: hence Moffatt's paraphrase of line 2: 'hot temper is the cause of many a sin.' Notice, in the last word, the Godward reference.

Line 1 repeats 15:18; *cf.* 14:17,29; 22:24,25.

29:23. Pride and humility

Cf. 16:18,19, and note.

29:24. Suicidal complicity

On the verse as a whole, *cf.* the dramatic sequence, 1:10-19.

Line 2: RV, 'he heareth the adjuration . . .'. *i.e.* his partnership involves him in the further sin of perjury (*cf.* Lv. 5:1). It is just possible that the proverb means: 'he is really partner with a thief who, being called on to testify, says nothing' (Hitzig, as summarized by Toy).

29:25. 'If God be for us . . .'

See note on 16:7. *Safe* is 'set on high' (*i.e.* beyond man's reach), an intensive form of the last verb of 18:10.

29:26. 'My expectation is from Him'

Favour is lit. 'face', which suggests more graphically the competition for, and expectations from, the personal notice of the man who makes the decisions. Yet such men are themselves the servants of appetites and pressures (*cf.* Acts 24:25-27), irrationality (1 Cor. 2:6,8) and instability (Ps. 146:3,4) which rob their interventions of all trustworthiness.

29:27. Birds of a feather

Common interests and mutual attraction at various levels may mask this enmity; nothing can mend it. In Solomon's own career his choice of partners revealed his actual choice of paths (1 Ki. 11). See 2 Corinthians 6:14-18.

V. WORDS OF AGUR (30:1-33)

This chapter owes its vividness largely to the author's profound humility, confessed in verses 1-9 and expressed both by his detestation of arrogance in all its forms and by his fascinated, candid observation of the world and its ways. In the groupings of men and creatures there is sometimes a moral or spiritual lesson stated or implied; but the lessons are nowhere pressed, and the dominant attitude is that of keen and often delighted interest, inviting us to look again at our world with the eye of a man of faith who is an artist and an observer of character. *Cf.* the words of the Psalmist: 'I muse on the work of thy hands' (Ps. 143:5, AV).

30:1-9. The sage looks upward
30:1. Agur son of Jakeh. 1 Kings 4:30,31 speaks of various sages besides Solomon. There is no need to find here (with Vulg.) a *nom-de-plume* for Solomon, requiring far-fetched interpretation. See Introduction, pp. 21ff.

The oracle (RV) correctly translates the Heb. *hammaśśā'*, and, if this is the true reading, emphasizes the authority of what follows. But RSV and most moderns assume a slight copyist's error, and read: *of Massa* (an Ishmaelite clan- or place-name: Gn. 25:14,16). This possibility is strengthened by the fact that in 31:1 the Heb. can be read this way as it stands; but the matter falls short of certainty.

To Ithiel, to Ithiel and Ucal (RSV): the Heb. consonants of this phrase can be revocalized to read: 'I have wearied myself, O God, I have wearied myself, O God, and come to an end', which introduces the opening theme well. The ancient versions likewise eliminate the proper names, but fail to agree in their translations. It remains an open question.

30:2-4. Man's worthless speculation. If in verse 2 there is an undertone of irony at the expense of the average man's self-assurance, verses 3,4 show that it springs from a pressing awareness of the ignorance and narrow experience of a mere human, and of the writer in particular. In his own way he affirms that reverence is the beginning of knowledge (*cf.* 1 Cor. 8:2).

Holy (3, AV) is plural and without the article, as in 9:10 (see note).

The echo (in 4) of the book of Job (*e.g.* chapter 38) is reinforced by the use of its characteristic form Eloah for God in verse 5. (See Introduction, p. 25.)

30:5, 6. God's flawless revelation. This follows hard on the preceding confession, answering its agnosticism.

Tried (RV) = smelted: they are without dross (*cf.* Ps. 12:6, 'as silver tried in a furnace . . ., purified seven times'), therefore there is no room left for our misgiving (5b) or for their improvement (6). Notice (5b) that the aim of revelation is to promote trust, not bare knowledge, and trust that goes behind the words to the Speaker.

30:7-9. Lead me not into temptation. The two requests, which converge on one goal, concern (a) character (8a), and (b) the circumstances that endanger character (8b,c,9). The prayer confirms the humility professed in verses 2ff., and unfolds it as (a) humility of ambition (a longing – *before I die* – for godly integrity, not for 'great things for (him)self'), and (b) humility of self-knowledge – for (as Toy points out) he might have prayed to use poverty or riches rightly, but knows his frailty too well.

30:10-33. The sage looks about him
30:10. Fairness for the unprivileged. This stands appropriately enough between the prayer of 7-9 and the portraits of 11-14, for arrogance (11) breeds oppression (14), while the fear of God (7-9) engenders respect for the weak. If the servant is innocent, his curse will count (*cf.* 26:2), for there is a Judge.

30:11-14. Four facets of arrogance. *Generation* (AV, RV) could perhaps be rendered 'circle' (D. W. Thomas).

The Heb. has no *there is . . .*; only a set of snapshots placed before the reader without comment, to display, full-grown, the arrogance prayed against in 7–9. There may be a sequence traceable from impious childhood (11) to practised brutality (14); at all events pride is seen corrupting a person's attitude to his superiors (11), himself (12), the world at large (13), and his supposed inferiors (14).

30:15, 16. Craving. The man of measureless ambition loses whatever lustre remains to him after verse 14, in this hungry company. The implied comparison is first comic, then tragic. '*Give! Give!*' can be taken as the names – with more pointed wit than as the cries – of these identical twins, who are made of the same stuff as their mother – other people's blood. But verse 16 leaves comedy behind, to reveal this craving as at once menacing (Sheol and the fire) and pathetic (the childless and the parched), and the reader of the two verses is left with mingled repulsion, fear and pity for human cupidity.

Three things . . ., yea, four . . .: see note on 6:16.

30:17. Nemesis for the arrogant. So the theme of the enormity of arrogance, which has dominated the chapter up to this point, is brought to its grim climax. It reappears briefly in verses 21–23, 32, 33.

30:18–20. Four marvels – and a jarring fifth. Some commentators, following Wisdom of Solomon 5:10,11, have sought a common denominator in the idea of movement which leaves no trace behind; but it would be better sought in that of the easy mastery, by the appropriate agent, of elements as difficult to negotiate as air, rock, sea – and young woman. The fifth, and unnatural, marvel (20) is that of a person utterly at ease and in her element in sin; an act of adultery is as unremarkable to her as a meal (20b,c). *So is the way . . .* (20, RV): the phrase refers not to 19, but back to 18: *i.e.*, 'likewise too wonderful for me . . .'

30:21–23. Four unbearable things. RSV rightly has *under*

three ...; *under four.* .... The Bible delights in fruitful reversals of
fortune (*cf.* 17:2; *cf.* the Magnificat), but has no use for upstarts
(*cf.* 19:10; Is. 3:4,5) who become too big for their boots. *Fool*
here is *nābāl*, the overbearing blasphemer of Psalm 14:1; *cf.* 1
Samuel 25:25; Proverbs 17:7,21. *Odious* (23, AV, RV) is lit.
'hated' or *unloved* (RSV); *cf.* Genesis 29:31. The implication may
be that she is naturally unpleasant (AV, RV), or that she is merely
old-maidish, and her success has gone to her head.

30:24-28. Four things little and wise. The four counter-
poises to weakness are (a) provision; (b) sanctuary; (c) order;
(d) audacity. Matthew Henry points out from this that we
should admire not bulk, *etc.*, but such qualities as appear here;
that we should wonder at the Maker of these small creatures;
blame ourselves for failing to 'act so much for our own true
interest as the meanest creatures do for theirs'; and 'not . . .
despise the weak things of the world'.

Conies (AV, RV; rock-badgers; Moffatt, more manageably, has
'marmots'): the Heb. term refers, it seems, to the *Hyrax Syriacus*,
a species of 'small mammals of a dull fawn colour . . ., about the
size of small rabbits' (Martin). They are shy creatures, quick to
retreat to their rock-crevices (*cf.* Ps. 104:18) at their sentry's
danger cry. *Spider* (AV): rather, *lizard* (RV, RSV). Either *taketh
hold, etc.* (AV, RV) or *you can take in your hands* (RSV) is a fair
translation; the latter is preferable, since (as Toy points out) in
the other three sayings the first line of each speaks of a limitation.

30:29-31. Four stately things. This passage, even more than
18-20, keeps (as the artist, *qua* artist, does) to the realm of
perception. There is no moralizing or philosophizing. The
theological implications (the Creator's power and wisdom – *cf.*
verses 1-5; Jb. 38-42:6) are left implicit, enriching the
observer's delight, if he has eyes to see, but not intruding upon it.

31. The second example is lit. 'the girt-of loins', which in
modern Hebrew means the starling (of all unlikely candidates,
with its bustling waddle). The ancient versions agree on the
barnyard *cock* (RSV) – certainly a noted strutter. *Greyhound*

(AV, RV) and *war-horse* (RVmg) are other nominees; but we have lost the key to the nickname. For the fourth example, 'A king whose army is with him' (*cf.* RVmg) is as likely a translation as any of the phrase 'a king *'alqûm* with him' (taking *'alqûm* as an Arabic loan-word (*cf.* our 'algebra', 'alcove') meaning 'the people' or 'the militia'). AV, RV strain grammar and syntax in inferring a lit. 'do not rise against him'.

30:32, 33. A concluding call to humility. Humility, the undercurrent of this chapter, which has already commended itself (directly or by contrast) as reverence (1–9), restraint (10–17) and wonder (18–31), is finally manifested as peaceable behaviour (32,33).

33. *Churning . . . wringing . . . forcing* (AV, RV) all translate one recurring word, *pressing* (RSV) or squeezing. W. M. Thomson[1] describes Arab women in Palestine vigorously wringing a large skin-bottle suspended from a tripod and full of milk, to produce a form of butter. The saying gains force from the close connection in Heb. between the words *nose* (*'ap̄*) and *anger* (*'appayim*).

VI. WORDS OF KING LEMUEL (31:1–9)

A king's calling

These verses take away the glamour from loose living (3–7), to exalt the glory of a king who is his people's protector (8,9). This is the context of verses 6,7, which are a cutting reminder that an administrator has better things to do than anaesthetize himself.

1. *Lemuel* was no king of Israel (unless the name – 'belonging to God' – is a *nom-de-plume*). The ancient versions give some support to RSV's *king of Massa* (see note on 30:1, under *The oracle*), and the language shows traces of foreign (but perhaps merely regional) dialect. The teaching is his mother's; but there is no hint that she was from Israel. See Introduction, pp. 24f.

2. The exclamations are affectionately reproachful: the king's

[1] *The Land and the Book*, 1910 edn., p. 235.

mother shames him by two things that he knows very well: that he matters to her (2a), and that she has vowed him to God (2b, *cf.* note on his name, verse 1). *Son*: the word (*bar*) is commoner in Aramaic than in Heb.; but *cf.* Psalm 2:12.

3. *To that which destroyeth* (AV, RV) is inaccurate; it is either 'so as to destroy', or, revocalized, *to those* (fem.) *who destroy* (so RSV).

4. The Heb. is cryptic, and many emendations have been suggested;[1] but G. R. Driver[2] translates it, with the consonants intact, 'Let there be (*'al*) no drinking . . .; And let there be no desiring (*'w* pointed *'awwō*) strong drink for rulers.'

6, 7. See summary of the section (1–9).

8. *Dumb* refers to those who cannot get a fair hearing. The last phrase of the verse is lit. 'sons of change', *i.e.*, the insecure.

VII. AN ALPHABET OF WIFELY EXCELLENCE

(31:10–31)

This acrostic is in all probability a distinct, anonymous section, rather than a continuation of the words of Lemuel's mother. In the LXX the latter are separated from the acrostic by five chapters (see Introduction, p. 25).

The subject of this portrait is a lady of some position, who has servants to manage (15c) and money to invest (16). As her husband's trusted partner (11) she has sole responsibility in her domain, which extends beyond the house to the management of her lands (16) and to dealings in the market, where she is as shrewd a seller (11,18,24) as a buyer (13,14). She treats her advantages not as a means to self-indulgence but as a widening of her responsibilities (27), for she is a tireless worker (15,18,19): there are the poor to help (20) and the vicissitudes of life to meet forearmed (21,25b). Yet with all her thrift, she is not austere (22), and with her business sense she is not hard, but a friend in need (20) and the delight of her children and her husband

[1] *Cf.* J. Gray, *The Legacy of Canaan*, 1957, p. 194 n.; D. W. Thomas, *VT*, 1962, p. 499.

[2] *Biblica*, 1951, p. 195.

(28,29). Her charm and her success (30,31) owe nothing to chance, because her outlook (30) and her influence (26) have the solid foundation of the fear and wisdom of the Lord.

Except in this last respect, this lady's standard is not implied to be within the reach of all, for it presupposes unusual gifts and material resources; nor is it much concerned with the personal relationships of marriage. Rather, it shows the fullest flowering of domesticity, which is revealed as no petty and restricted sphere, and its mistress as no cipher. Here is scope for formidable powers and great achievements – the latter partly in the realm of the housewife's own nurture and produce (31); and partly in her unseen contribution to her husband's good name (23).

10. *A virtuous woman* (AV, RV): better, 'a fine wife' (*cf.* 12:4). The Heb. *ḥayil* denotes, in different contexts, strength, wealth, ability (*cf.* 'mighty man of *valour*').

15. *Portion* (AV) or *task* (RV, RSV): either is possible. The word means 'what is appointed'.

16. *Fruit of her hands*: *i.e.*, the money her hands have earned: *cf.* verses 13,24.

19. *Distaff*: the meaning of the Heb. word, found only here, is conjectural. G. R. Driver[1] argues for the sense 'the mending'.

21. *Scarlet*: if this is the right translation, the point will be that it denotes high cost. She can afford the best, and by implication, the fully adequate. But the word has a plural ending, which is abnormal for 'scarlet'; so that both form and sense arouse suspicion. The consonants allow the reading *double* (AVmg), *i.e.*, double thickness, which is supported by Vulg. and LXX (the latter joining it to the next verse). This reading, leaving the consonantal text undisturbed, is altogether preferable to Toy's ingenious expedient of making 22a follow 21a, and 21b follow 22b (so that 21 would speak of warmth, and 22 (reading 'scarlet') of elegance). This is unsupported, and would also dislocate the acrostic.

26. *Kindness*: *ḥesed*; see note on 21:21.

30. *Favour* (AV, RV): better, *charm* (RSV). See note on 11:16.

[1] *JTS*, 1922, p. 407.

A SHORT CONCORDANCE

to the Authorized Version of The Proverbs

Abomination
yea, seven are an abomination unto him 6:16
A false balance is abomination to the Lord 11:1 (*cf.* 20:23)
The sacrifice of the wicked is an abomination to the Lord 15:8; 21:27 (*cf.* 28:9)

Acknowledge
In all thy ways acknowledge him 3:6

Angry (see also **Wrath**)
Make no friendship with an angry man 22:24 (*cf.* verse 25)
An angry man stirreth up strife 29:22 (*cf.* 15:18)

Ant
Go to the ant, thou sluggard 6:6
The ants are a people not strong 30:25

Beginning
The fear of the Lord is the beginning 1:7; 9:10
The Lord possessed me in the beginning 8:22
The beginning of strife is as when one letteth out water 17:14

Boast
but when he is gone his way, then he boasteth 20:14
Whoso boasteth himself of a false gift 25:14
Boast not thyself of to morrow 27:1

Brother
See subject-study: The Family, III, p. 52.

Chasten, Correct
See subject-studies: Wisdom, I(1), p.36; The Family, II, p. 50.
despise not the chastening of the Lord 3:11

Child
See subject-study: The Family, II, pp. 50ff.
Even a child is known by his doings 20:11

Counsel
They would none of my counsel 1:30
Where no counsel is, the people fall 11:14 (*cf.* 15:22; 20:18)
the counsel of the Lord, that shall stand 19:21 (*cf.* 21:30)
the sweetness of a man's friend by hearty counsel 27:9

Dead, Death
See subject-study: Life and Death, pp. 53ff.

Discretion
See subject-study: Wisdom, I(3),(4), pp. 36f.

Dog
As a dog returneth to his vomit, so a fool ... to his folly 26:11
like one that taketh a dog by the ears 26:17

185

Eat

When thou sittest to eat with a ruler 23:1

eat so much as is sufficient for thee 25:16

and eateth not the bread of idleness 31:27

End

See references in commentary on 5:4

Enemy

he maketh even his enemies to be at peace with him 16:7

Rejoice not when thine enemy falleth 24:17

If thine enemy be hungry, give him bread to eat 25:21

but the kisses of an enemy are deceitful 27:6

Entice

if sinners entice thee, consent thou not 1:10

Envy

Envy thou not the oppressor 3:31 (*cf.* 23:17)

but who is able to stand before envy? 27:4 (*cf.* 14:30)

Eyes

Let thine eyes look right on 4:25

the ways of man are before the eyes of the Lord 5:21 (*cf.* 15:3)

All the ways of a man are clean in his own eyes 16:2

the eyes of a fool are in the ends of the earth 17:24 (*cf.* 27:20)

who hath redness of eyes? 23:29

Fall

a just man falleth seven times, and riseth up again 24:16

Rejoice not when thine enemy falleth 24:17

Whoso diggeth a pit shall fall therein 26:27 (*cf.* 28:10)

Father

See subject-study: The Family, II, pp. 50ff.

Fear

The fear of the Lord is the beginning 1:7; 9:10 (*cf.* 15:33)

Be not afraid of sudden fear 3:25

A wise man feareth, and departeth from evil 14:16

Better is little with the fear of the Lord 15:16

The fear of man bringeth a snare 29:25

Fire

Can a man take fire in his bosom 6:27

Where no wood is, there the fire goeth out 26:20 (*cf.* verse 21)

and the fire that saith not, It is enough 30:16

Folly, Fool

See subject-study: The Fool, pp. 39ff.

Friend

See subject-study: The Friend, pp. 44ff.

Gift

A wicked man taketh a gift out of the bosom 17:23 (*cf.* 29:4)

A man's gift maketh room for him 18:16 (*cf.* 19:6; 21:14)

Glory

The hoary head is a crown o. glory 16:31 (*cf.* 17:6; 20:29)

it is his glory to pass over a transgression 19:11

It is the glory of God to conceal a thing 25.2

to search their own glory is not glory 25:27

God
See subject-study: God and Man, pp. 31ff.

Gold
My fruit is better than gold 8:19
As a jewel of gold in a swine's snout 11:22
The fining pot is for silver, and the furnace for gold 17:3; 27:21
A word fitly spoken is like apples of gold 25:11

Harlot (see also **Woman**)
he that keepeth company with harlots spendeth his substance 29:3 (*cf.* 6:26)

Hate
How long . . . will . . . fools hate knowledge? 1:22 (*cf.* 8:36)
The fear of the Lord is to hate evil 8:13 (*cf.* 13:5; 15:27)

Hear
He that answereth a matter before he heareth it 18:13
The hearing ear, and the seeing eye, the Lord . . . made . . . both 20:12

Heart
Trust in the Lord with all thine heart 3:5
Keep thy heart with all diligence 4:23
The heart knoweth his own bitterness 14:10
A merry heart maketh a cheerful countenance 15:13 (*cf.* 15:15; 17:22)
Who can say, I have made my heart clean 20:9
The king's heart is in the hand of the Lord 21:1

Hell
See subject-study: Life and Death, pp. 53ff.

Honeycomb
For the lips of a strange woman drop as an honeycomb 5:3
The full soul loatheth an honeycomb 27:7

Honour
Honour the Lord with thy substance 3:9
Lest thou give thine honour unto others 5:9
and before honour is humility 15:33; 18:12
It is an honour for a man to cease from strife 20:3
so honour is not seemly for a fool 26:1 (*cf.* verse 8)

Hope
Hope deferred maketh the heart sick 13:12
but the righteous hath hope in his death 14:32

House
her feet abide not in her house 7:11
Wisdom hath builded her house 9:1
Every wise woman buildeth her house 14:1
Prepare thy work . . . and afterwards build thine house 24:27
yet make they their houses in the rocks 30:26

Instruction
See subject-study: Wisdom, 1 (1), pp. 36f.

King
By me kings reign, and princes decree justice 8:15
It is an abomination to kings to

commit wickedness 16:12 (*cf.* verses 10–15)

Mercy and truth preserve the king 20:28 (*cf.* 29:4,14)

The king's heart is in the hand of the Lord 21:1

the heart of kings is unsearchable 25:3 (*cf.* verses 1–6)

The locusts have no king 30:27

nor thy ways to that which destroyeth kings 31:3

Knowledge
See subject-study: Wisdom, 1(5), p. 37.

Labour
In all labour there is profit 14:23 (*cf.* 13:11; 16:26)

Landmark
Remove not the old landmark 23:10

Law
See references in commentary on 3:1

Life
See subject-study: Life and Death, pp. 53ff.

Light
the path of the just is as the shining light 4:18

the commandment is a lamp; and the law is light 6:23

Lips
See subject-study: Words, pp. 46ff.

Lord
See subject-study: God and Man, pp. 31ff.

Lot
The lot is cast into the lap 16:33 (*cf.* 18:18)

Love
and be thou ravished always with her love 5:19

let us take our fill of love 7:18

I love them that love me 8:17 (*cf.* verse 36)

but love covereth all sins 10:12 (*cf.* 17:9)

Better is a dinner of herbs where love is 15:17

Open rebuke is better than secret love 27:5

Lowly (see also **Proud**)
but he giveth grace unto the lowly 3:34

but with the lowly is wisdom 11:2

Message, Messenger
As the cold of snow in . . . harvest, so is a faithful messenger 25:13

He that sendeth a message by the hand of a fool 26:6 (*cf.* 10:26)

Multitude
In the multitude of words there wanteth not sin 10:19

in the multitude of counsellers there is safety 11:14; 24:6 (*cf.* 15:22)

In the multitude of people is the king's honour 14:28

Name
but the name of the wicked shall rot 10:7

The name of the Lord is a strong tower 18:10

A good name is rather to be chosen than great riches 22:1

Neighbour
See subject-study: The Friend, p. 44.

Debate thy cause with thy neighbour himself 25:9

Net

Surely in vain the net is spread in the sight of any bird 1:17

A man that flattereth his neighbour spreadeth a net for his feet 29:5

News

As cold waters . . . so is good news from a far country 25:25

Ox

Where no oxen are, the crib is clean 14:4

a stalled ox and hatred therewith 15:17

Path (see also **Way**)

acknowledge him, and he shall direct thy paths 3:6

But the path of the just is as the shining light 4:18

Peace

Her ways are ways of pleasantness, and all her paths are peace 3:17

but to the counsellors of peace is joy 12:20

he maketh even his enemies to be at peace with him 16:7

Pit

See **Fall**; also **Woman**

Poor (see also **Rich**)

He that oppresseth the poor reproacheth his Maker 14:31 (*cf.* 17:5)

Better is the poor that walketh in his integrity 19:1 (*cf.* 28:6)

All the brethren of the poor do hate him 19:7 (*cf.* 14:20)

He that hath pity upon the poor lendeth unto the Lord 19:17 (*cf.* 28:27)

The rich and poor meet together 22:2

Poverty

So shall thy poverty come as one that travelleth 6:11

give me neither poverty nor riches 30:8

Prayer

but the prayer of the upright is his delight 15:8 (*cf.* verse 29)

He that turneth away . . ., even his prayer shall be abomination 28:9

Pride

Only by pride cometh contention 13:10

Pride goeth before destruction 16:18 (*cf* 17:19; 29:23)

Proud

A proud look, a lying tongue 6:17

Better . . . than to divide the spoil with the proud 16:19

Prudent

See subject-study: Wisdom, 1(4), p. 37.

Rebuke, Reproof

See subject-study: Wisdom, 1(1), p. 36.

Recompense

The righteous shall be recompensed in the earth 11:31

Say not thou, I will recompense evil 20:22

Rich, Riches (see also **Poor, Poverty**)

The rich man's wealth is his strong city 10:15; 18:11

The blessing of the Lord, it maketh rich 10:22

Riches profit not in the day of wrath 11:4

There is that maketh himself rich, yet hath nothing 13:7

riches certainly make themselves wings 23:5

he that maketh haste to be rich shall not be innocent 28:20 (*cf.* verse 22)

Righteous, Righteousness (see also **Wicked**)

but righteousness delivereth from death 10:2; 11:4

righteousness exalteth a nation 14:34 (*cf.* 16:12; 29:2)

Better is a little with righteousness 16:8

but the righteous are bold as a lion 28:1

Rod

See subject-study: The Family, II, pp. 5of.

A whip for the horse ... and a rod for the fool's back 26:3 (*cf.* 19:29)

Rubies

wisdom is better than rubies 8:11

a virtuous woman ... her price is far above rubies 31:10

Scorner

See subject-study: The Fool, III, pp. 41f.

Secret

but his secret is with the righteous 3:32

bread eaten in secret is pleasant 9:17 (*cf.* 20:17)

A talebearer revealeth secrets 11:13; 20:19

Open rebuke is better than secret love 27:5

Servant

the fool shall be servant to the wise of heart 11:29

A wise servant shall have rule over a son that causeth shame 17:2 (*cf.* 14:35)

He that delicately bringeth up his servant 29:21

Accuse not a servant unto his master 30:10

(the earth is disquieted ...) For a servant when he reigneth 30:22 (*cf.* 19:10)

Shame

shame shall be the promotion of fools 3:35

When pride cometh, then cometh shame 11:2

He that answereth ... before he heareth ..., it is folly and shame 18:13

Simple

See subject-study: The Fool, I, p. 39.

Sin

See subject-study: God and Man, pp. 31ff.

Fools make a mock at sin 14:9

sin is a reproach to any people 14:34

Who can say, ... I am pure from my sin? 20:9

The thought of foolishness is sin 24:9

He that covereth his sins shall not prosper 28:13

Sleep

See subject-study: The Sluggard, pp. 42f.

thou shalt lie down, and thy sleep shall be sweet 3:24

they sleep not, except they have done mischief 4:16

Love not sleep, lest thou come to poverty 20:13

Slothful, Sluggard

See subject-study: The Sluggard, p. 42f.

Son

See subject-study: The Family, II, pp. 50ff.

Sorrow, Sorrowful

and he addeth no sorrow with it 10:22

Even in laughter the heart is sorrowful 14:13

Soul

he that doeth it destroyeth his own soul 6:32 (*cf.* 8:36; 29:24)

The liberal soul shall be made fat 11:25 (*cf.* 13:4; 22:9)

he that winneth souls is wise 11:30

A true witness delivereth souls 14:25

Whoso keepeth his mouth . . . keepeth his soul 21:23

Spirit

and he that ruleth his spirit than he that taketh a city 16:32 (*cf.* 25:28)

but a wounded spirit who can bear? 18:14 (*cf.* 15:13; 17:22)

The spirit of man is the candle of the Lord 20:27

Surety

if thou be surety for thy friend 6:1

Sweet, Sweetness

(she saith to him) Stolen waters are sweet 9:17 (*cf.* 20:17)

The desire accomplished is sweet to the soul 13:19

to the hungry soul every bitter thing is sweet 27:7

the sweetness of a man's friend by hearty counsel 27:9

Thief

Men do not despise a thief, if he steal . . . when he is hungry 6:30

Whoso is partner with a thief hateth his own soul 29:24

Tongue

See subject-study: Words, pp. 46ff.

a soft tongue breaketh the bone 25:15

in her tongue is the law of kindness 31:26

Trust

Trust in the Lord with all thine heart 3:5

He that trusteth in his own heart is a fool 28:26 (*cf.* 11:28)

The heart of her husband doth safely trust in her 31:11

Understanding

See subject-study: Wisdom, I(2), p. 36.

Vinegar

As vinegar to the teeth, . . . so is the sluggard to them that send him 10:26

as vinegar upon nitre, so is he that singeth . . . to an heavy heart 25:20

Way

He . . . preserveth the way of his saints 2:8

but the way of transgressors is hard 13:15

There is a way that seemeth right unto a man 14:12; 16:25 (*cf.* 12:15)

When a man's ways please the Lord 16:7

how can a man then understand his own way? 20:24

Train up a child in the way he should go 22:6

and the way of a man with a maid
30:19

Weight
but a just weight is his delight
11:1 (*cf.* 16:11)
Divers weights . ... are . . .
abomination to the Lord
20:10,23

Wicked (see also **Righteous**)
the expectation of the wicked
shall perish 10:28
the tender mercies of the wicked
are cruel 12:10
The sacrifice of the wicked is an
abomination to the Lord 15:8
yea, even the wicked for the day
of evil 16:4
the candle of the wicked shall be
put out 24:20
The wicked flee when no man
pursueth 28:1
when the wicked rise, a man is
hidden 28:12,28 (*cf.* 29:2,8,12,
16,18)

Wife
See subject-study: The Family, I,
pp. 49f.

Wine
Wine is a mocker, strong drink is
raging 20:1
Look not thou upon the wine
when it is red 23:31
it is not for kings to drink wine
31:4
Give . . . wine unto those that be
of heavy hearts 31:6

Wisdom
See subject-study: Wisdom,
pp. 36ff.

Witness
See references in commentary on
14:5

Woman
To deliver thee from the strange
woman 2:16 (*cf.* 7:5; 22:14;
23:27,28)
so is a fair woman which is without discretion 11:22
a virtuous woman 12:4; 31:10
Every wise woman buildeth her
house 14:1
a brawling (or, a contentious)
woman 21:9,19; 27:15
an adulterous woman . . . saith,
I have done no wickedness 30:
20
Give not thy strength unto
women 31:3

Word
See subject-study:Words, pp. 46ff.
Every word of God is pure: . . .
Add thou not unto his words
30:5,6

Wounds
The words of a talebearer are as
wounds 18:8; 26:22
Faithful are the wounds of a
friend 27:6

Wrath
A fool's wrath is presently known
12:16 (*cf.* 27:3; 29:11)
He that is slow to wrath is of great
understanding 14:29 (*cf.*
14:17; 16:32)
A soft answer turneth away
wrath 15:1
so the forcing of wrath bringeth
forth strife 30:33